Breaking

Down

Silos:

Innovation in
Dual Diagnosis Systems

Brandi Braud Kelly, PhD, MCP

Dedication

This book is dedicated to my sister, Kati Marie Braud. She is my light in this world and has led me throughout my career. When I feel defeated, frustrated, or just plain tired, I remember all the challenges Kati has faced throughout her life and all that she and others with challenges like hers will continued to encounter if the rest of us don't persevere.

Thank you, Kati, for inspiring me and everyone you meet.

Table of Contents

Tables/Figures

Tables

Figures

Acknowledgements

While I have encountered many people throughout my career who have inspired and challenged me, I would like to take the time to thank a few very special people without whom I would not have completed this publication.

From a professional perspective, three key individuals must be mentioned. First, I would like to thank Dr. Johnny Matson for introducing me to this intriguing, challenging, and rewarding work. I had the opportunity to study and learn from him early in my career and without that experience would have likely taken a very different career path. Johnny, thanks for helping me to "see the light." Since my initial education and training, I have been fortunate to work with two very important colleagues. Drs. Jay Sevin and Amy Greer have served as both friends and colleagues. They have been my sounding board for ideas and frustrations throughout my career and the process of this book.

Professional accomplishments are never possible without a strong personal support system. I would like to thank my parents, Dwight and Debbie Braud, for always believing in me and challenging me. You guys never let me settle for the easy way out and that has served me well throughout the years. I want to thank my sister, Jodi Braud Molliere, for being my companion on the journey not only with our family but in our work both together and individually to make the lives of people with disabilities better and brighter. I am blessed to have you as both a sister and a colleague. I want to thank my boys, Cole and Jacob, for always making me smile and inspiring me to do bigger things than I believed possible. You are both inspirations to me, and I am proud to be your mom. Finally, I want to thank my husband, Michael, for being by my side throughout this process. I could not do any of the work before me without your love and support.

Executive Summary

Individuals with intellectual and developmental disabilities may experience co-occurring behavioral health conditions similar to those experienced by individuals without disabilities. Recognition of such needs and access to appropriate treatment is essential to achieving positive outcomes and successful living and work within the community. Despite efforts across states and professional organizations, needed behavioral health services and supports remain fragmented, unsustainable, or unavailable, with many recipients and families left waiting until the next crisis occurs.

This book will examine both clinical and system's issues that impact assessment, diagnosis, and treatment of behavioral health challenges for individuals with IDD. It will examine not only clinical and professional issues, but systems, regulations and fiscal impacts on supports and services available to individuals and their families. Systems issues are not intended to focus solely on state or federal entities or programs. The system(s) that serve and support these individuals include all people and entities with a "stake" in their lives. Systems discussions will consider a variety of approaches and entities.

Chapter 1 will provide an overview of dual diagnosis including review of history, prevalence, national approaches, and challenges. Chapters 2-5 will present other contextual and system issues contributing to the challenges navigating and accessing services and the typical system silos recipients and families may experience will be reviewed. Chapters 6-9 will provide recommendations to enhance existing system successes as well as needed changes to ensure access to services and positive health and life outcomes for individuals with dual diagnoses. Chapter 10 will provide a summary of concluding comments and core components to implementing recommendations.

Chapter 1

Diagnostic Overshadowing: Have We Really Left it Behind?

Today the presence of co-occurring behavioral health diagnoses for individuals with intellectual and developmental disabilities (IDD) is openly acknowledged by professionals with expertise and experience supporting individuals with IDD. However, acceptance within the general behavioral health community varies, often depending upon the exact nature and experience of the professional an individual with IDD encounters.

Appropriate recognition of separately presenting behavioral health conditions for individuals with IDD impacts health outcomes for these individuals. Recognition of co-occurring behavioral health conditions when present provides a clearer path for treatment and support decisions which in turn lead to better outcomes for the individual. Known evidence-based approaches and modifications to practices within the general behavioral health arena result in effective management of symptoms and improvements in quality of life. Behavioral health challenges left untreated remain a primary variable leading to institutionalization and disruption of community living/work for individuals with IDD.

The first step in improving outcomes for individuals with co-occurring IDD and behavioral health needs centers on recognition of co-occurring conditions. We must move past the idea that an individual's IDD is the genesis of all challenges and needs or negates the need for access to appropriate behavioral health treatment. This chapter will review the historical changes in diagnosis of behavioral health needs for individuals in IDD as well as discuss challenges that remain. Prevalence of co-occurring diagnoses will be reviewed along with challenges in establishing accuracy of estimates. A review of current state service trends will be presented. Finally, the chapter will summarize significant contextual challenges that shape the environment in which federal, state and private entities must function to support individuals with co-occurring conditions.

Historical Overview of Dual Diagnosis and Diagnostic Overshadowing

The presence of behavioral health issues for individuals with developmental disabilities was first acknowledged in the 1960s (Borthwick-Duffy, 1994; Myrbakk & vonTetzchner, 2008; Reiss, 1990; Reiss & Szysko, 1983). Prior to this time it was believed that any mental health or behavioral challenges present for someone with an intellectual/developmental disability (IDD) was in fact related to the person's IDD. The term "diagnostic overshadowing" was first used by Reiss and colleagues in the early 1980s to describe the tendency to attribute behavioral health symptoms to an individual's disability (Reiss, 1982; Reiss & Szysko, 1983). This diagnostic overshadowing was highlighted with the emerging recognition of comorbid conditions, although it continued to a degree of significance for some time. Even professionals who work with persons with IDD weren't immune to diagnostic overshadowing and disagreement across professionals further complicated the diagnostic picture (Jacobstein, Stark, & Laygo, 2007; Reiss & Szyszko, 1983; Sevin, Bowers-Stephens, & Crafton, 2003). Review of records in clinical practice often reveals that many individuals with behavioral health needs have received a lengthy list throughout their lifetimes of often conflicting diagnoses and no clear delineation of symptom presentation or targets. It is rare to find a thorough review of differential diagnoses or an attempt to clarify the confusing history often presented.

More accurate diagnoses and recognition of behavioral health needs occurred with improvements in assessment that emerged with the development of psychopathology scales for individuals with IDD in the 1980s (Esbenson, Rojahn, Aman, & Ruedrich, 2003; Marston, Perry & Roy, 1997; Matson & Bamburg, 1998; Matson, Gardner, Coe, & Sovner, 1991; Matson & Shoemaker, 2011; Matson & Williams, 2014; Mindham & Espie, 2003; Mohr, Tonge, & Einfeld, 2005; Moss et al., 1997; Moss et al., 1998; Reiss, Levitan, & McNally, 1982; Reiss, Levitan & Syzsko, 1982; Reiss & Valenti-Hein, 1994; Rojahn, Matson, Lott, Esbensen, & Smalls, 2001). Traditional approaches to diagnostics focus heavily on interview of the "patient" and the person's ability to self-report symptoms and answer questions. The cognitive and communication challenges many individuals with IDD experience may preclude reliance on this type of evaluative activity. Individuals with IDD may communicate in nonverbal methods, have difficulties with understanding questions asked, and/or challenges in communicating effectively even when able to do so verbally. Communication of more abstract concepts such as mood and anxiety may be even more challenging for some individuals with IDD. Some individuals may also be predisposed to response bias. For example, they may typically and consistently respond in the affirmative or negative to closed-ended questions that attempt to obtain symptom endorsement or lack thereof. Additionally, many typical psychopathology scales are not designed to account for the impact of the individual's IDD versus a possible co-occurring behavioral health need and may not support the report of other caregivers/family members when needed. Individuals with IDD may present symptoms somewhat differently than those without IDD. Examples of diagnostic symptoms that may present differently can be seen in Table 1.

Table 1. Example of Symptom Presentation Differences

Symptom Category	IDD Presentation Considerations/ Possible Behavioral Indicators
Anxiety	Avoiding eye contact and looking down Shaking Rubbing/wringing hands Pushing others away Remaining in bedroom or area away from others Aggression or SIB when confronted with PTSD triggers
Depression	Irritability may be more prominent throughout lifespan Crying with no obvious trigger Avoiding of activities (or "noncompliance")
Mania	Increased behavioral challenges Walking as if driven Inability to sit still Sexual acting out
Psychosis	Nonsensical comments atypical from the norm Picking at skin/clothing Withdrawal atypical from the norm Eye and head movements as if hearing something not present (when no seizure disorder is present)

Due to these noted challenges, scales that were developed focused more specifically on the following to more accurately screen for possible psychopathology:

1. Symptom variations that could be directly observed or fairly easily inferred from behavioral presentations or groupings of behavioral symptoms,

2. Symptoms or diagnostic characteristics that could not be attributed to the IDD, but instead were more indicative of a possible additional comorbid behavioral health condition, and

3. Differential symptom presentations based on data from research studies and known expert consensus statements/guidelines.

The majority of these behavioral health assessment tools are not designed as specific diagnostic scales per se; rather they aid the clinician in identification of possible diagnostic considerations and areas in need of further exploration (Charlot & Beasley, 2013; Myrbakk & von Tetzchner, 2008). The most widely recognized scales developed and often used today are presented in Table 2.

Table 2. IDD Diagnostic Screening Instruments

Instrument	Author(s)	Published Date(s)	Description
Reiss Screen for Maladaptive Behavior	Reiss	1987; Internet version now available	· 38 items · Parent/caregiver report · Scales: aggression, autism, avoidant disorder, dependent personality disorder, depression, paranoia, psychosis, drug abuse, hyperactivity, self-injury, sexual problems, stealing, suicidal tendencies · 3 primary indices: severity of challenging behavior, psychiatric diagnosis, rare but significant problems · Significant rating on 1 scale suggests need for referral for full evaluation
Reiss Scales for Children's Dual Diagnosis	Reiss & Valenti-Hein	1988; internet version now available	· 60 items · Parent/caregiver report · Scales: anger/self-control problems, attention deficit, autism/PDD, conduct disorder, depression, poor self-esteem, psychosis, somatoform disorder, withdrawn-isolated behavior, crying spells, enuresis/encopresis, hallucinations, involuntary movements, pica, sexual problems, lying, setting fire, verbally abusive · 3 primary indices: severity of challenging behavior, psychiatric diagnosis, rare but significant problems · Significant rating on 2 scale suggests need for referral for full evaluation
Psychopathology Instrument for Mentally Retarded Adults (PIMRA)	Matson	1984	· 56 items · Parent/caregiver report · Respondent version available · Scales: Schizophrenia, affective disorder, psychosexual disorder, adjustment disorder, anxiety disorder, somatoform disorder, personality disorder, inappropriate adjustment · Significant rating on any scale suggests need for referral for full evaluation
Diagnostic Assessment for the Severely Handicapped-II (DASH-II)	Matson	1995	· 84 items · Parent/caregiver report · Designed for individuals with severe to profound cognitive challenges · Scales: anxiety, depression, mania, PDD/autism, schizophrenia, stereotypies, self-injurious behavior, elimination, eating, sleeping, sexual, organic, impulse control · Ratings address frequency, severity, and duration of presenting symptoms · Significant rating on any scale suggests need for referral for full evaluation

Assessment for Dual Diagnosis (ADD)	Matson & Bamburg	1998	· 79 items · Parent/caregiver report · Designed for individuals with mild or moderate cognitive challenges · Scales: mania, depression, anxiety, post-traumatic stress disorder, substance abuse, somatoform disorders, dementia, conduct disorder, PDD, schizophrenia, personality disorders, sexual disorders, eating disorders · Ratings address frequency, severity, and duration of presenting symptoms · Significant rating on any scale suggests need for referral for full evaluation
Psychiatric Assessment Schedule for Adults with Developmental Disabilities (PAS-DD)	Moss and colleagues	1997; Mini version and checklist developed in 1998	· 145 items · Scales: schizophrenia and other psychotic disorders, bipolar disorder, depression, phobic and anxiety disorders, obsessive compulsive disorder, autism spectrum disorders, personality disorders · Recipient and parent/caregiver reporting options · Can be completed by a "non-professional" · Linked to ICD diagnoses · Ratings focus on symptoms/behaviors within the past 4 weeks
Clinical Behavior Checklist for Persons with Intellectual Disabilities (CBCPID)	Marston, Perry, Roy	1997	· 30 items · Linked to ICD diagnostically · Assesses depression symptoms and challenging behaviors
Behavior Problems Inventory (BPI)	Rojahn, Matson, Lott, Esbenson, Smalls	2001	· 52 items · Parent/caregiver report · Frequency and severity ratings applied · Aimed at evaluating self-injurious behavior, stereotypic behavior, and aggressive/destructive behavior
Anxiety, Depression and Mood Scale (ADAMS)	Esbenson, Rojahn, Aman, Ruedrich	2003	· 28 items · Parent/caregiver report · 5 subscale: Manic/hyperactive behavior, depressed mood, social avoidance, general anxiety, compulsive behavior
Developmental Behavior Checklist for Adults (DBC-A)	Mohr, Tonge, Einfeld	2005	· 107 items · Parent/caregiver report · Focus on rating emotional and behavioral symptoms not attributable to IDD
Glasgow Anxiety Scale for People with Intellectual Disabilities	Mindham & Espie	2003	· 27 items · Designed for use with recipients; completed by healthcare professionals · Produces a total Anxiety Score with 3 subscales: worries, specific fears, and physiological symptoms

Along with the growing recognition of behavioral health needs for individuals with IDD, professionals working with individuals with IDD began using the term "dual diagnosis" to refer to a comorbid diagnosis of IDD and behavioral health condition (Reiss & Szyszko, 1983). A further challenge in overcoming the diagnostic overshadowing phenomenon links back to more common usage of the "dual diagnosis" term, notably to refer to individuals with a behavioral health condition and substance abuse/use need. In fact, a basic internet search of the term without the accompanying reference to developmental disabilities will exclusively pull up information related to behavioral/mental health and substance abuse. In encounters with clinicians and providers outside of the intellectual and developmental disability arena, the assumption of dual diagnosis using this latter reference continues to be the primary interpretation today. Variations on the use of the term with an understanding of the different comorbid groupings that may be included are unique to professionals and providers with specialization and experience supporting individuals with IDD.

Prevalence of Mental Health Conditions for Individuals with Intellectual and Developmental Disabilities (IDD)

It is generally accepted within the intellectual and developmental disabilities field, that the prevalence of behavioral/mental health needs in IDD is not only consistent with, but greater than that within the general population. Estimates vary across publications, although commonly cited estimates are that approximately 20-70% of individuals with IDD have a comorbid behavioral health need (Barnhill & McNelis, 2012; Borthwick-Duffy, 1994; Dekker & Koot, 2003; Holden & Gittleson, 2003; Iverson & Fox, 1989). The National Core Indicators data gathered across states via support from the National Association of State Directors of Developmental Disability Services indicates that approximately 32.4% of individuals receiving services for IDD also present with behavioral health needs (NASDDDS, 2013). Numerous challenges remain to obtaining a more consistent and replicable prevalence estimate. Depending upon study approach, setting, and definition of "behavioral health" prevalence varies from 7-97% (Charlot & Beasley, 2013; Cooper, Smiley, Morrison, Williamson, & Allan, 2007).

Often different criteria or definitions are employed across studies. Studies using a more typically accepted definition consistent with an existing diagnostic nomenclature tend to result in lower prevalence rates compared to those using an adapted diagnostic nomenclature such as the *Diagnostic Manual for Intellectual Disabilities* (DM-ID) or *Diagnostic Criteria-Learning Disability* (DC-LD) (Fletcher, Loschen, Stavrakaki, & First, 2007; Royal College of Psychiatrists, 2001). Without adaptation, individuals with significant emotional/behavioral needs may go undiagnosed and more importantly untreated simply due to the challenges in reporting and recognition of some symptoms due to the impact of the person's IDD (Barnhill, 2003; Barnhill & McNelis, 2012; Charlot & Beasley, 2013; Deb, Holt, & Bouras, 2004; Sovner, 1986). As previously noted, traditional diagnostic systems rely heavily on self-report of symptoms, and many symptoms are not observable or easily inferred when the individual is unable to discuss or confirm them. Table 3 provides example of common diagnostic categories and associated symptoms that are challenging to establish in individuals with limited communication abilities. While publications of guidelines and adaptations such as DM-ID and DC-LD have assisted in improving diagnostic recognition, generally practicing professionals are not familiar with this information. Thus, it remains limited in terms of distribution and application.

Table 3. Diagnostic Challenges in DSM-5

Diagnosis	Symptoms Difficult to Observe without Self-Report OR to tease out IDD impact
Schizophrenia	Delusions
	Hallucinations
Manic Episode	Inflated self-esteem or grandiosity
	Flight of ideas or subjective experience thoughts are racing
	Distractibility
Major Depressive Episode	Feelings of worthlessness
	Diminished ability to think or concentrate or indecisiveness
	Recurrent thoughts of death
Generalized Anxiety Disorder	Excessive anxiety or worry
	Individual finds it difficult to control worry
	Difficult concentrating or mind going blank
Obsessive-Compulsive Disorder	Recurrent and persistent thoughts, urges, or images that are experienced as unwanted or intrusive
	Individual attempts to ignore or suppress thoughts, urges, or images or to neutralize them
	Use of compulsions that "individual feels driven to perform in response to obsession"
Posttraumatic Stress Disorder	Recurrent, involuntary and intrusive distressing memories of the traumatic event
	Recurrent distressing dreams related to traumatic event
	Dissociative reactions
	Intense or prolonged distress at exposure to internal or external cues
	Inability to remember aspects of traumatic event
	Negative expectations or beliefs about oneself/others/world
	Distorted cognitions
	Feelings of detachment or estrangement from others
	Inability to experience positive emotions
	Problems with concentration

The use of different criteria or definitions is further compounded by variations in instruments or methods of diagnosis applied (Charlot & Beasley, 2013). Studies may use a particular assessment tool in isolation to determine presence or absence of symptoms sufficient for diagnostic assumption. Others rely on existing diagnoses rendered within an individual's health record. Still others use a varied approach of instruments, record review, and "expert" determination to look for convergence of information supportive of diagnoses. These differences significantly impact comparability of information and add to the widely variant estimates.

Sample characteristics of studies also impact results. Studies vary greatly in terms of living situation (home versus institution), age of individuals, level of intellectual disability, and type of developmental disability (Cooper et al, 2007). Reference to other studies for comparison purposes often do not account for these differences, making interpretation difficult. Living situation may impact results since individuals residing in institutional situations may be more likely to present with behavioral/mental health challenges given the relationship between these factors. Individuals with more significant behavioral health needs are more likely to be admitted to institutional settings creating a sample bias (Braddock et al., 2015). Age differences exist in term of age of onset and symptoms presentation (American Psychological Association, 2013). Developmental expectations change as an individual ages; thus, some emotional reactions may be normative for youth but not for an adult. Additionally, some diagnoses are known to present in the developmental period while others occur more often in adulthood. Age of participants will impact the resulting prevalence estimates particularly when specific diagnostic conditions are examined. Disability type and severity may also impact symptom reporting and presentation. Given that challenges in problem solving and coping skills increase with increasing cognitive challenges, it would be expected that rate of diagnosis of co-occurring behavioral health needs would increase. However, the more significant an individual's cognitive and communication skills, the more difficult assessment and recognition become. Tie these challenges to use of diagnostic nomenclature often based on self-report and establishing a clear prevalence rate becomes even more difficult.

A final variable exerting considerable impact on prevalence estimates surrounds the inclusion or exclusion of individuals with "behavioral challenges" who may not have a separate diagnosed behavioral health condition (Cooper et al., 2007). Within the intellectual and developmental disability field, most professionals are less driven by diagnostic confirmation as the primary factor in determining need for treatment. That is, while diagnosis may improve some understanding of presenting symptoms and factors that need to be considered and may assist in directing treatment, diagnosis to treatment match is only one among a number of variables to consider in developing a comprehensive support plan for an individual. Within the field it is widely understood that treatment must be individualized and account for the variety of factors impacting that individual's behavioral presentation of which a diagnosis may be only one. A related consideration is the interrelationship between behavioral health diagnoses and behavioral challenges. As with other diagnostic overshadowing biases, professionals may assume if a diagnosis is present, then it accounts for the behavioral presentation, or they may miss a diagnosis by over-focusing on the behavioral presentation. Research indicates that behavioral challenges may exist within the context of the mental health condition or that the two may exist for the same individual but the mental health condition may be only one of many factors impacting the behavioral presentation (Baker, Blumberg, Freeman, & Wiessler, 2002; Rojahn, Matson, Naglieri, & Mayville, 2004) Additionally, professionals with expertise in this area understand that individuals with behavioral challenges even in the absence of a traditional behavioral health diagnosis often need professional behavioral health services. Minimally, a comprehensive assessment should be completed to assist the support team in determining next steps in treatment and support. Particularly in instances where the individual has a complex set of needs crossing professional boundaries and/or has limited communication skills, an appropriately experienced behavioral health professional must lead the evaluation of medical, genetic, psychological, environmental, and developmental needs and contributants (Barnhill & McNelis, 2012; Charlot & Beasley, 2013). Families and staff supporting the individual will not be equipped to sort through the complexity of issues with which many of these individuals present. Determination surrounding inclusion of this group of individuals significantly impacts estimates of needed professional services in some instances resulting in prevalence estimates as varied as 10.1% when only traditional behavioral health diagnoses and approaches are considered and 45% when behavioral challenges are included for the same population of individuals (Grey, Pollard, McClean, MacAuley, & Hastings, 2014). Emerson (1995) highlighted that any behavior that places the "physical safety of the person or others in serious jeopardy or is likely to seriously limit use of or be denied access to ordinary community facilities" warrants being a focus of treatment. Thus, regardless of diagnostic label, behavioral challenges identified as meeting this criteria should be linked to some behavioral health service which supports that focus on the higher percentages may more accurately predict demand and need for professional services.

State Service Trends

Given the challenges noted in recognizing behavioral health need for individuals with IDD, access to needed behavioral health services and supports has historically been a challenge for individuals with IDD (Beasley & duPree, 2003; Emerson, 1995; US Department of Health and Human Services, 2005; US Public Health Services, 2002). Despite efforts throughout the last several decades, barriers to access remain. The National Association of State Directors of Developmental Disability Services (NASDDDS) 2014 mid-year conference focused explicitly on the area of Dual Diagnosis highlighting a general consensus that supporting the behavioral health needs of individuals with IDD remains a significant challenge across the nation. Accessing needed behavioral health services via the traditional behavioral health programs/options remains a significant gap in services and supports for these individuals across most states years after this challenge was first noted. To address the significant gaps in services, some states have implemented and invested in varied strategies with some success including contracting with experts to implement Systemic Therapeutic Assessment Resources and Treatment, building a separate behavioral health infrastructure and expertise within their IDD system, implementation of rules/regulations requiring risk identification and crisis planning, cross program collaborative efforts, and specialized options from the state University Center(s) of Excellence in Developmental Disabilities (UCEDDs). Figure 1 illustrates the breakdown of these various state efforts.

Figure 1. State Trends in Service Settings

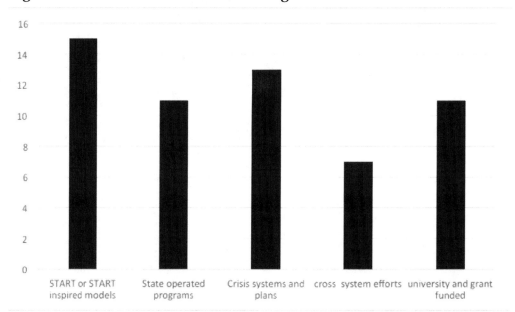

*NOTE: two UCEDDs partner in the states START program and these were only counted in the START numbers to avoid duplication

Systemic Therapeutic Assessment Resources and Treatment

Fifteen states within the United States have implemented Systemic Therapeutic Assessment Resources and Treatment (START) models or programs based within the START principles (Charlot & Beasley, 2013; Beasley & duPree, 2003; Beasley & Hurley, 2007; Beasley & Kroll, 2002). Core components of this model focus on systematic and comprehensive assessment, provider capacity and education, linkage and coordination, and short-term crisis and respite services. Local coordinators and teams support the recipients and draw on consultation from state and national experts. Positive outcomes of these programs include decreased use of high cost services such as emergency room services and hospitalizations, decreased need for admission to more restrictive and perhaps more costly institutional settings, and greater community involvement (Charlot & Beasley, 2013). Challenges that remain include capacity and continued waiting lists for services, consistency of support by provider staff and family, and access to needed acute services when warranted. Additionally, the bulk of the services provided within this model do not have typical funding stream options and are funded via state general funds or Medicaid waiver service options necessitating commitment of funds which states may or may not have each year depending on current economic issues.

State Staffed and Funded Options

Eleven states operate at least some state staffed and state funded programs specifically for individuals with intellectual/developmental disabilities and co-occurring behavioral health needs (Moseley, 2003; Moseley, 2012). Operation of such programs provides for direct oversight and direction of these programs by the

State Office or Division of Developmental Disabilities. Clinicians with specific experience and expertise in serving individuals with dual diagnosis as well as with the person-centered practices embedded within most IDD systems are hired within these programs. The focus of most programs is typically two-fold: Direct service provision of behavioral health services to those with complex needs and outreach/liaison with community providers and professionals to assure linkage to needed supports as well as opportunities to build the capacity of these organizations and professionals to support individuals with a dual diagnosis. These programs represent positive efforts to fill gaps and ensure needed services to individuals, but to date no clear outcomes/evidence is available to demonstrate transfer of expertise to community providers or professionals in a manner that may decrease the need for dedicated state programs to address these needs.

Crisis Planning

Required crisis planning represents another strategy employed by some states to improve collaboration and response to intensification of needs for individuals with intellectual disabilities and behavioral health needs (Moseley, 2004; Moseley, 2012). Currently, thirteen states employ some form of required crisis planning. Variability exists in how plans are completed and responsibility and collaboration differ significantly. In some instances the developmental disability office/division is responsible for completing planning, while in others the behavioral health office/division plays this role. Still others lay out a more equally shared role across offices. Benefits of the crisis planning model include clear identification of crisis triggers and symptom cues along with planning for actions to be taken to address emerging crisis issues and responsibility for each action. This approach is clearly consistent with accepted guidelines in the field that support the benefits of planning ahead for crisis response (Beasley & duPree, 2003). However, it represents only one component of planning for needed behavioral health services and only begins to achieve needed integration processes when multiple systems/services are implicated. Additionally, these approaches focus exclusively on state operated developmental disability and behavioral health programs and expectations which represent only a portion of the systems and programs with which an individual with IDD interfaces.

Cross Systems Efforts

In many states individuals must seek services via different programs with separate requirements and processes. (Chapter 4 will provide more details about complex systems and programs individuals and their families may navigate.) Current cross systems efforts in some states involve state required expectations across the developmental disability office/division and the behavioral health office/division. Roles for each office/division are outlined inclusive of responsibilities and funding agreements where applicable. Seven states utilize some formal cross systems programs or planning (Moseley, 2004; Moseley, 2012). These efforts focus on one of two typical options. Some states specifically operate discrete cross systems programs such as inpatient/residential units which are staffed and funded via shared resources across the state offices/divisions. Others outline expectations for cross office planning and provision of support. This second approach would require sharing of information and a single plan of care/support that includes services accessed and funded via each office/division and shared planning and coordination. Cross systems efforts provide for at least some acknowledged shared responsibility and coordination of services for individuals who present for support from both systems. Applicability and availability for individuals not seeking services and funding via the state operated systems is not clear. Additionally, current efforts do not address the multiple systems individuals may encounter such as education, social services, or non-governmental options.

University Centers for Excellence in Developmental Disabilities

University Centers for Excellence in Developmental Disabilities (UCEDDs) have been in existence since 1963, and currently each state and United States territory has at least one designated UCEDD designed to act as a resource for expertise in supporting individuals with disabilities with eleven states having 2 or 3 UCEDDs (Association of University Centers on Disability, 2011). Core functions of UCEDDs are noted to include:

1. Preservice preparation for recipients and families

2. Technical assistance and community education

3. Research

4. Information dissemination

Authorization for UCEDDs currently generates from Public Law 106-402, the Developmental Disabilities Assistance and Bill of Rights Act (2000), while funding derives from a number of governmental sources with oversight from the Administration on Intellectual and Developmental Disabilities (Association on University Centers on Disability, 2011). UCEDDs may partner with federal, state, and local governments and programs to carry out core functions and implement special projects.

A focus on dual diagnosis is not a requirement for each UCEDD and significant variation exists across states in terms of primary areas of focus. The most well recognized UCEDD focused on dual diagnosis issues is the Nisonger Center at the University of Ohio (The Ohio State University Nisonger Center, 2014). This program represents a true center of excellence in dual diagnosis and partners in significant program development and research with the existing state programs and private organizations. Work associated with the Center is further supported by shared grants with the state. Most UCEDDs hire or contract with psychologists or social workers, although they may work in a variety of early intervention, clinical treatment, and/or administrative functions. A much smaller number of UCEDDS have specific projects or programs focused on Autism Spectrum Disorders, Positive Behavior Supports, Applied Behavior Analysis, Dual Diagnosis, or Substance Abuse services. An even smaller number focus on training for professionals or direct support workers for individuals with behavioral health needs. Figure 2 provides an overview of efforts across states.

Figure 2. UCEDD Dual Behavioral Health Efforts

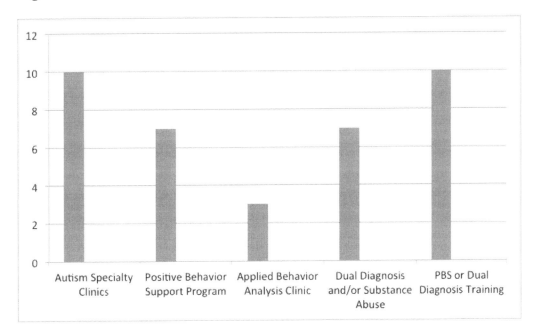

Contextual Challenges

The previous section highlights the variability across states in approach to addressing the needs of individuals with dual diagnosis. It is likely that a multi-faceted approach is needed to truly address the challenges and gaps in meeting the needs of individuals with these co-occurring needs. To begin to conceptualization what may be necessary and the complexity of thinking needed to address the challenges, it is necessary to gain an understanding of the contextual issues and challenges that must be considered. This section will review the most significant issues impacting any approach to successfully supporting individuals with dual diagnosis.

Funding and Fiscal Impacts

Recent fiscal challenges on a national level have necessitated changes across states inclusive of cuts to programs and services available to individuals with disabilities similar to those experienced within other governmental areas and consistent with historical changes often resulting in cuts to needed programs, services, and supports (Beasley & duPree, 2003; Dorfman & Awmiller, 2003; Moseley, 2012; Thaler, Moseley, Cooper, and LeBeau, 2008). Even with recovery potentially in sight in some states, the reality is that economical resources will wax and wane with other factors, and as such the dependence of the support system for individuals with IDD and behavioral/mental health needs on governmental funding will determine the cyclical changes the system experiences.

Deinstitutionalization and the Advent of HCBS

As individuals have moved out of institutional settings, home and community based service providers have been challenged to serve those they have not previously supported and in some instances are not always ready to serve. Individuals historically served in one system may now need services from another. Debate regarding the right of individuals with developmental disabilities to receive support to live and work within their local communities has faded from the discussion. However, the debate has moved to the practicalities of providing the needed supports for each individual. In the early days of the home and community based advocacy efforts, the push for funding and support in this arena was clearly and firmly planted in the civil rights forum. Initial funding occurred in 1981 and was designed to support and assist families in continuing to support their loved ones to remain at home and in their communities (Lakin, Doljanic, Taub, Chiri, & Byun, 2007). The purpose was to avoid the historical institutionalization of individuals simply on the basis of a diagnosis of IDD and to move away from the idea that the presence of the disability was the defining feature of the individual. Prior to this movement, most individuals with developmental disabilities resided in institutional settings and professionals typically recommended institutionalization as "the best" option for a family.

As deinstitutionalization has continued, individuals with more complex needs are moving to community living situations and are in need of supports (Charlot & Beasley, 2013; Lakin et al, 2007). These challenges are magnified as the move to home and community based services has spread to the more traditional behavioral/mental health systems. Individuals were previously supported within contexts in which multiple disciplines work on site day to day. While conditions in institutional settings have historically been questionable in terms of rights, privacy, and choice, the ability to coordinate and share high cost professional services across multiple individuals with similar needs represented a rarely considered convenience. As individuals moved to home living situations, planning for needed supports did not always calculate adequately the complex support needs and challenges in coordinating these in multiple locations across individuals or the cost of providing them individually. Examples of complexities that may challenge a community based support system and require flexible and atypical support planning approaches can be found in table 4.

Table 4. Complexities Challenging Community Support Systems

Complex Support Profile/Issues	Challenges
Individual with relatively minor support needs for typical daily living needs but with diagnosis of borderline personality disorder	• Frequent staffing changes throughout day more challenging but may be necessary • Professional oversight of interventions as often as needed • Professional support for support staff to sustain the challenges daily and consistently implement needed intervention strategies
Individuals with anticipated needs for crisis services	• Quick access to crisis services by professionals familiar with the individual and his/her needs
Individual with a dual diagnosis who needs medication, behavioral strategies, and instructions for family/staff support	• Coordination of medication changes/needs with implementation of behavioral strategies • Clear guidelines on which professional to seek when problems occur • Consistency in instructions to family/staff across professionals
Individual with significant medical issue and co-occurring behavioral health need	• Coordination and prioritization of needed medical interventions when behavioral issues may impact cooperation • Coordination of needed medication changes and impact on behavioral presentation and strategies

Workforce Challenges

A general projected workforce shortage looms ahead for all Medicaid support based programs. Most professionals report minimal interest in serving those individuals reliant on Medicaid for health care coverage. When looking at general mental health needs, fifty-five percent of Americans live in US counties with no psychiatrist, psychologist, or social worker (Substance Abuse and Mental Health Services Administration, 2013). New or expanded services may further strain the mental health system in general which enhances these problems. Increased coverage either in expanded populations for existing services or implementation of newly covered services will increase the number of individuals seeking services resulting in increased demand in an already strained system.

Cross System Interactions

Individuals with IDD often interface with multiple systems, and those with co-occurring needs may in many states already interface with, minimally, two systems, one addressing developmental disability needs and one addressing mental health needs (Brookman et al, 2009; Dorfman & Awmiller, 2003; Jacobstein et al., 2007). Understanding across systems and ease of navigation across systems for recipients and their families is a key factor in meeting needs effectively. Professionals and staff in other service systems often mistakenly assume that the IDD service system does and/or should have all service and support options for individuals with IDD. Based on this assumption, when IDD is suspected or confirmed the expectation is often for the IDD system to provide all needed supports. When the IDD system is unable to meet the various needs, the individual becomes like a hot potato bouncing across systems (Dorfman & Awmiller, 2003; Jacobstein et al., 2007). The problems may be worsened when individuals or their families present within a court situation, and the judge is equally unfamiliar with the various service systems and options. Systems rarely set requirements necessitating not only superficial collaboration in the form of discussions and meetings but also actual planning to pull together support options, resources and funding across multiple areas within various programmatic systems and providers. In the most challenging instances, recipients and their families may find themselves denied eligibility for services within one system due to the symptoms that qualify for another (Jacobstein et al., 2007). When this application of exclusionary criteria occurs in its most severe form, the individual may be unable to receive almost any service from any program. These challenges may be further exacerbated when individuals and families receive no services or must wait significant periods of time to receive services, particularly when all or most available services require meeting eligibility for Medicaid funded services. Families not meeting Medicaid eligibility may be faced with the need to have one parent cease working, or parents may divorce so that financial eligibility becomes a possibility. While access to services may occur more speedily, the erosion of the family unit and/or the loss of family resources negatively impact the child's overall support system and creates a cycle of more demand on an already stressed funding stream. Similarly, parents may face loss of guardianship or willing abdication of it simply to access needed assistance. The result further magnifies negative impact on the child and the system as well as increasing the number of programs now needing to coordinate to serve a single child/family.

Developmental and Aging Challenges

Many services within typical medical and behavioral health programs (irrespective of funding stream) stop at adulthood. Many parents cite this loss of service as a major change in continuity of support for their child, and it can have a significant impact on the health outcomes for the child and the ability of the family to continue to offer needed supports within the home setting (McMorris, Weiss, Cappelletti, & Lunsky, 2013). Federal mandates for many programs and private insurance often require the provision of "medically necessary" services to youth. These services cover, as implied, a wide array of needed services for individuals meeting program requirements, including personal care supports, allied health treatments, dental services, and behavioral health supports. Programs that provide needed preventive health and mental health services or that offer temporary out of home treatment options which are often a bridge between more acute treatments and a longer term institutionalization options may also only be available to youth.

Considering the impact a developmental disability may have on an individual's needs throughout his/her lifespan, services that for those without an IDD may be reasonable to stop in adulthood may for this group of individuals have a significant and perhaps life altering impact if halted. Even within the youth years, modification to approaches may be required. Individuals with IDD who receive support from their state developmental disability system, often do so with some degree of paid staff supports. Some programs allow for family therapy and training options but do not include similar options for staff. Where we believe family involvement is needed, likely staff involvement may need to be considered. Training for families and staff may be a lifelong consideration for some individuals with IDD.

Summary

This chapter has reviewed the historical issues related to dual diagnosis, provided a discussion of prevalence and need for behavioral health services, reviewed existing strategies implemented across the nation, and summarized key contextual issues that must be considered. The issues and needs surrounding individuals with dual diagnoses are clearly quite complex. Effective strategies for addressing the needs of individuals with dual diagnoses must be equally complex and must consider all of the issues presented within this chapter. The next several chapters will review other key issues and challenges not traditionally highlighted in dual diagnosis discussions but significantly impacting the success of supporting individuals with co-occurring needs. Chapter 6 begins the discussion of recommendations and solutions to breaking down silos and implementing innovations in dual diagnosis systems.

Chapter 2

Early Intervention Principles:
Are They Really Only for the Young?

Early intervention services typically refers to supports across multiple professional disciplines occurring in early childhood between ages 0 to 5 (Division of Early Childhood Education, 2014). While the idea of "intervening early" may be discussed and used to a degree in many other situations, these early childhood years are recognized as needing a clear focus on risk for developmental delay such that individual and family-specific interventions can be designed and implemented to mitigate risk.

The purpose of early intervention programs centers on several key outcomes including the following (Dunst & Trivette, 2009):

1. Support and strengthen the caregiver's competence and confidence,

2. Promote and enhance children's competencies, and

3. Optimize a child's learning and development

Individuals with IDD often require supports across many life areas. Accessing needed supports relies on a combination of family and paid supports to provide guidance and assistance. Early intervention services are planned and designed to support and guide the support system for the greatest generalization and maintenance of gains in skills and independence. Because early intervention can mitigate against later needed supports, early intervention programs are aimed at remediating existing challenges as well as preventing those for which the individual may be "at risk" of developing (Division of Early Childhood Education, 2014). This focus allows some children to experience gains that result in acquiring skills and independence commensurate with their same age peers by the end of the early intervention period, thus removing a need for ongoing specially designed supports. For those who do not gain skills similar to same age peers, the early efforts often result in a lessening of needed supports and maximizing of independence.

Early intervention services must be provided consistent with the requirements outlined in the Individuals with Disabilities Education Act (IDEA, 2004). The IDEA outlines the following key principles:

1. Professionals must identify disabilities and challenges as well as risks for developing further challenges.

2. Additional practice and specific strategies are needed to assist individuals with disabilities.

3. A team based approach that coordinates across all disciplines and programs must be implemented.

4. Interventions best occur in naturalistic situations.

5. Family centered approaches must be implemented.

6. Outcomes must be identified, measured, and used in further planning efforts.

This chapter will focus on some of the key principles and requirements implemented within early intervention programs, review their positive impact within the early intervention field, and examine which may assist in more success throughout the lifespan if continued beyond the typical early intervention ages.

Team-Based Approach

Team-based approaches to support involve identification of all involved professionals and support staff as members of a team with the recipient and his/her natural support system. Much of the IDD field uses at least some degree of team-based planning. However, early intervention represents the most well described area of team function and activities. While various models exist to support the team based approach expected in early childhood, the federal guidelines for early intervention programs clearly spells out expectations for the team approach (Division of Early Childhood Education, 2014). Requirements of note include the following:

1. All professionals must work as a team to complete assessments and ongoing outcomes reviews.

2. Professionals must build partnerships with the family in supporting the child and work together to determine outcomes/goals and develop the plan.

3. Professionals must coordinate and work together to implement the agreed upon plan.

4. Professionals communicate and share information and expertise to build capacity of other team members and the family.

5. All team members, including professionals, engage in shared problem-solving.

In addition to the clearly noted expectations, the acknowledged best practice approaches of the primary service provider model and the transdisciplinary model both set very high standards for team coordination and collaboration not typically seen in other parts of most systems/programs (Dunst & Trivette, 2009). Benefits of explicit team based approaches such as these go beyond the obvious improved coordination and integration across disciplines. With a well implemented team based approach, outcomes are improved and duplication of services is avoided (Adams & Tapia, 2013; Division of Early Childhood Education, 2014; Dunst & Trivette, 2009). Figure 3 depicts common team-based approaches including primary service provider and transdisciplinary models.

Figure 3. Early Intervention Support Models

Multidisciplinary Approach: Individual professionals working side by side and sharing information.

Interdisciplinary Approach: Individual professionals working together to assess, plan and support.

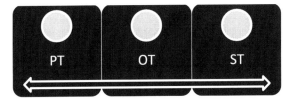

Transdisciplinary Approach: Professional working in synergistic relationships learning from one another and sharing roles across professionals.

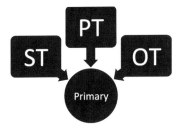

Primary Service Provider Model: Professionals working as a team with a lead provider facilitating and coordinating.

Elements of team expectations can be found throughout the IDD service. However, as the child leaves the early intervention system, the core team tends to get smaller, often only involving the recipient, family (at least in childhood years) and the in-home/residential provider. Additionally, multiple teams can be seen in most recipients' lives beyond the core support team for typical IDD services including the following:

1. School teams geared toward development of the Individual Education Plan (IEP) and school-based supports

2. Medical teams or in many cases various medical professionals who minimally (if at all) interact to coordinate care but do offer recommendations that impact support across other areas

3. Behavioral health teams or professionals providing recommendations

Most IDD programs set at least some expectations that support coordinators/case managers within their systems must gather information from these others sources or "teams" and may encourage inclusion of these other individuals/teams on the core support team. In the author's experience typically no requirements for participation or inclusion are in place, and compensation and resources for the needed involvement may be missing. HCBS requirements require that a case manager be involved in the evaluation, plan development, and monitoring process for all HCBS services (Centers for Medicare and Medicaid Services, 2014b). Additionally, the case manager must ensure the plan covers all areas of need, services across programs, and that needed referrals for services in other programs occur. These guidelines do not provide for how any coordination and collaboration beyond referral would occur and do not define required membership of participation within a team based approach outside of the case manager, recipient, and family (if applicable). Regulation within Intermediate Care Facilities for Individuals with Intellectual/Developmental Disabilities (ICF/IDDs) identify that a Qualified IDD Professional similar to a case manager must facilitate the individual's plan of support and that the individual, family (if applicable), and support staff must participate in planning and implementation (Centers for Medicare and Medicaid Services, 2015). Professional participation in the planning and implementation is vague, stating only that "professionals must participate in relevant aspects." Requirements for general Medicaid services for youth via the Early Periodic Screening Diagnosis and Treatment (EPSDT) include offering a case manager to the recipient and family but does not require one nor are there any stated requirements for coordination or collaboration across professionals/providers supporting the same youth (Rosenbaum, 2008). No case management function is required or routine in adulthood. This author could find no requirements for team based services or coordination and collaboration across professionals within private insurance options. For many individuals with IDD and co-occurring behavioral health issues, the need for integration and coordination across family, school, and other professional services does not go away simply as a function of age. The team-based expectations included in early intervention practices offer a guide to integration and collaboration throughout the lifespan for people with complex needs.

Naturalistic Training and Caregiver Support

Like with the team-based approach, a focus on naturalistic training is a cornerstone of early intervention programs (Division of Early Childhood Education,

2014; Dunst & Trivette, 2009; Jennings, Hanline & Woods, 2012). Providers of early intervention services begin with the expectation that services will be provided in the settings in which the child and family live their lives. These settings include the home, school/early childhood center, neighborhood parks/playgrounds and other community places. Services do not occur within a more typical clinic setting without a significant justification as to why they are not able to be provided within a natural environment. One commonly adopted method of addressing the provision of services in the child's natural environment involves routines-based interventions. In routines-based interventions, the provider(s) look at the environments within which the child spends his/her time and the typical activities that occur within these environments so that a plan can be developed to "embed" the needed interventions into typical activities (Jennings et al., 2012). The Division of Early Childhood Education (2014) lays out several key expectations for learning in the natural environment including:

1. Interventions occur in "natural and inclusive" environments to maximize learning opportunities.

2. Universal design principles must be used in planning interventions.

3. Appropriate environmental adaptations must occur.

4. Learning opportunities must occur within the context of normal routines and activities.

Using these types of techniques ensures that interventions occur naturally in the course of a child's day and activities, at a frequency that allows many opportunities for learning, and in conjunction with parents, teachers, and other supports. Generalization and maintenance of any skill learned or behavioral change is maximized. Given the cognitive and communication challenges some individuals with IDD experience and the impact behavioral health challenges may have across all life activities, taking advantage of naturalistic approaches to intervention and support would seem to remain an important component for all individuals with IDD regardless of age. For individuals requiring a significant amount of support and guidance throughout the day and across many activities, learning occurs more readily when paired with the activities and situations in which the new skill or coping mechanism is expected to be displayed. This approach also allows for greater generalization across situations and maintenance of the skill when the more formal, professional supports may fade.

Closely tied to the idea of training within the natural environment, support for the family and other caregivers marks an important expectation within the early intervention system (Division of Early Childhood Education, 2014; Dunst & Trivette, 2009; Jennings et al., 2012). Parents, teachers and other caregivers spend a great deal of time with children and interact with them frequently throughout each day in various situations and activities that offer a wide array of opportunities for the child to learn important skills or continue practicing those that are problematic. It is unrealistic to expect small and infrequent opportunities within a more traditional clinic-based setting to achieve the same intensity of change for these children. Conversely, expecting a professional or set of professionals to construct and implement a set of interventions that occur frequently throughout the child's day would be quite costly. Thus, the best model of intervention revolves around the early intervention professionals mentoring and coaching parents/teachers and other caregivers to implement interventions within the already discussed natural settings (Division of Early Childhood Education, 2014; Dunst & Trivette, 2009; Jennings et al., 2012).

Similar to other areas discussed, clear expectations are laid out for the involvement and coaching of families/caregivers (Division of Early Childhood Education, 2014).

1. The family, teacher, and other caregivers are part of the child and family support team.

2. Early intervention professionals must address within the planning and implantation processes the family's "concerns, priorities, and changing life circumstances."

3. The family is intimately involved in setting outcomes and goals for the child.

4. Planning supports the family and builds family competence in supporting the child.

These family centered practices along with inclusion of other important caregivers in the child's life result in shared goals and improved and more consistent implementation of effective strategies (Dunst & Trivette, 2009; Jennings et al., 2012). When caregivers are supported in their efforts and are coached to use effective interventions, the child gains are less dependent on paid and/or expert resources. Thus, sustainability of supports and gains associated with intervention strategies is improved. Many individuals with IDD and co-occurring behavioral health needs continue to rely on family and other support throughout their lives. Thus, ability to support inclusion of the family and other caregivers in all aspects of planning and implementation along with the benefits of this approach would seem obvious as a key feature of support expectations. This approach should not be viewed as taking away from the focus on independence. Each person should be supported to be as independent as possible and to guide his/her support planning process, including determination of who the individual wants as part of his/her support plan. Those individuals identified by the individual as part of their support plan will need guidance, involvement, and support. For individuals continuing to receive supports related to their IDD, there will be by definition supports offered and needed with regard to at least some aspects of daily life, work, and community. The type and intensity of supports should be based upon each individual's need but will be different from that expected for individuals without IDD as they move through adolescence and adulthood. The recommendation to support inclusion of family and staff is not designed to remove the individual's independence, but rather to support the support system identified for each individual. Individuals whose independence allows for minimal support may not need intense involvement from family and staff.

Focus on Outcomes

A final important component within early intervention systems involves the use of data and the focus on child outcomes. The primary purpose of early intervention services is to identify individuals with developmental delay AND at risk for delay and implement intensive and early interventions to mitigate the risk. Thus, typical early intervention programs include routine collection of data on child progress with specific goals and objectives, routine review of the data and progress so that modifications can occur as needed, and program reporting of child outcomes to assess success or lack thereof in meeting benchmarks for percentage of children improving and percentage assessing consistent with same age peers at discharge (Division of Early Childhood Education , 2014; Dunst & Trivette, 2009; Individuals with Disabilities Education Act, 2004; Jennings et al., 2012).

While all IDD support programs contain at least some components of monitoring and outcomes, most fall short of what is seen in early intervention systems. Typical IDD data and outcomes requirements have focused more on process indicators over outcomes more specifically related to improvements and changes for the recipient that have a real impact on quality of life. Incorporation of data and outcomes monitoring and clear linkage to not only individual progress determinations but also program evaluation would allow for better understanding of programs and supports that work and those that do not, ultimately leading to improved systems. As with other issues discussed in this chapter, this issue and its importance should not be unique to early intervention services or needs.

Summary

This chapter has covered core components of early intervention programs and requirements as well as identification of potential impact of loss of such components as each child ages out of the early intervention model. Additionally, the chapter begins to highlight the multiple systems that begin to lead to the fragmentation in supports as a child leaves the early intervention system. These issues must be reviewed and addressed beyond early intervention to avoid a fragmented and siloed approach. Chapter 6 will offer recommendations related to addressing many of these issues, while Chapter 9 will focus on improvements in support and training for families and caregivers.

Chapter 3

What Happens Here Stays Here:
Is School Las Vegas?

Intellectual and developmental disabilities are typically diagnosed during childhood; thus, school involvement becomes crucial. School systems must provide support to individuals with IDD as well as those with emotional/behavioral challenges (IDEA, 2004). School must identify needs consistent with IDEA definitions and categories, and for those who meet criteria must provide supports, accommodations, and treatment for noted needs. While this requirement adds potential support options, it may also further complicate navigation, coordination, and receipt of the appropriate services and supports. The IDEA notes several key outcomes which are important in addition to the principles already shared in Chapter 2 (IDEA, 2004). The purpose of IDEA includes the following:

1. Ensure that all children regardless of disability receive a public education,

2. Ensure protection of rights of all children, and

3. Provide guidance to assist state and local education agencies to provide needed services to children with identified needs

Families who believe their children may meet requirements for specialized supports and accommodations, via IDEA, can request an interdisciplinary evaluation to determine eligibility (IDEA, 2004). Similarly, teachers may make such referrals. Following the evaluation, the school is required to develop an Individualized Education Plan (IEP) to address all identified needs from the evaluation. Like early intervention requirements, a team approach is used in the development of the IEP; however, unlike the early intervention program approach, the team-based approach within the education system most often includes only school-related personnel/professionals, the child, and the family. The focus of the IEP is on the school environment and the child's educational needs (IDEA, 2004). For children receiving services from other programs or professionals, the challenges of coordination across the school system and other programs/services can be difficult. The next chapter will focus on the complexities and challenges of the multiple systems that individuals and families must navigate beyond the school. Since school is such an integral part of youth learning and support, this chapter will focus on the unique issues within the school system and how that may impact the totality of supports an individual must access irrespective of the number of other systems/ programs involved.

School Diagnostic Systems

The federal Department of Education sets guidance and rules related to IDEA, while each State's Department of Education sets state requirements and works with local school districts to align special education services consistent with the Individuals with Disabilities Education Act (IDEA, 2004). These services within the educational arena cross IDD, behavioral health, and physical/medical disability needs. For individuals who do not engage the system within an early intervention program, often school is the initial place within which a possible disability is recognized. School documents, evaluations, and IEPs are often used in historical review of information to establish diagnoses and eligibility for services in other systems/programs. While this historical information is quite helpful in many instances, it can serve to complicate the diagnostic and eligibility issues. Several complexities must be considered in understanding the challenging interplay between these systems.

The criteria in IDEA which guide the eligibility criteria for special education services are not tied to recognized diagnostic nomenclature and may be different than the required eligibility for IDD and behavioral health services. The criteria is not necessarily inconsistent with a specific diagnosis as recognized clinically or in other systems; however, similar to the broad based approaches to eligibility in early intervention programs, the school systems often provide a broader set of criteria or more room for clinical judgment and use of nonspecific categories of disability (National Dissemination Center for Children with Disabilities, 2014). Diagnosis and eligibility become important as a gateway to service and support options; thus, problems and inconsistencies in identification in this realm can result in lack of access to needed services or erroneous access to inappropriate services. Disability categories are established via IDEA (2004) rather than diagnoses per se and are as follows: 1) Autism. 2) Deaf-Blindness, 3) Deafness, 4) Developmental Delay, 5) Emotional Disturbance, 6) Hearing Impairment, 7) Intellectual Disability, 8) Multiple Disabilities, 9) Orthopedic Impairment, 10) Other Health Impairment, 11) Specific Learning Disability, 12) Speech or Language Impairment, 13) Traumatic Brain Injury, and 14) Visual Impairment. A small number of these categories are titled similar to actual diagnoses including Autism and Intellectual Disability; however, the descriptions of these categories do not require adherence to the diagnostic indicators within any particular scheme (i.e., DSM or ICD). Other categories such Developmental Delay, Emotional Disturbance, Orthopedic Impairment, and Multiple Disabilities may link or be associated with diagnoses but are broad descriptions that would cover multiple diagnoses. Still others such as Specific Learning Disability and Speech or Language Impairment are more specific to academic challenges and associated conditions but may not be linked to either developmental disability or mental health diagnoses.

The varied diagnostic and eligibility schemes across the educational and other systems can mean that a child identified as needing supports for developmental or learning disabilities in one system may not be identified in that manner in another system. Similar challenges can occur with the identification for emotional/

behavioral needs. The broader approaches within the educational system can be viewed as a normal and desired extension of the early intervention approaches that occur prior to official school enrollment. That is, providing some intensive and specialized services to a greater number of children who meet some criteria of risk that impacts their educational and social skills may result in better outcomes, more independence, and less need for services over time. This approach actually makes sense from the perspective of a focus on ensuring youth with any possible disability are identified early, and services and support are put into place to ensure the best academic outcomes for each student. Increased academic outcomes lead to greater education and independence later in life and less need for outside support or dependence on others. The challenge comes into play when inconsistencies occur across systems. Parents and teachers understandably have expectations that a child found eligible in one system would similarly be determined eligible in another related system, particularly when identification of reported disability has a similar category noted in each system. For the children who may achieve optimal outcomes and need minimal to no assistance outside of the school environment, the approach seems to work. For those with more complex and persistent challenges who need a greater degree of services typically lasting throughout the lifespan, the need for consistent identification and coordination across systems can be impaired due to the different schemas used across settings.

An additional complicating factor may occur if a full assessment is not completed with all identified needs included in a comprehensive plan. In the author's experience, a child's noted disability qualification in the academic environment may be driven more by the most prominent presenting issue/needs. A child with very significant IDD-related needs is more likely to be identified as meeting eligibility for services via an IDD-related condition and to have related diagnoses and IDD support needs clearly noted in his/her IEP. On the other hand, a child with very significant behavioral health needs will more typically have a related emotional/behavioral diagnosis and associated needs in his/her IEP. References to other needs may or may not be clearly outlined in the plan, and often other possible diagnoses or conditions are not assessed for and recognized in the document. When children then present for eligibility to other systems/programs, the incomplete documentation may lead to incorrect assumptions and determinations. Table 5 offers comparison of key diagnostic schemas used across systems.

Table 5. Diagnostic Model Comparisons

Model	DSM-5	ICD-10	DM-ID	IDEA
Key Features	Mental Health Diagnoses and Criteria Guidelines for specificity Research, support and prevalence background information	Medical diagnoses and coding Billing specifiers for each diagnosis	Modifications to Mental Health Diagnoses and criteria for individuals with IDD Guidelines for specificity Research, support, and prevalence background information for individuals with IDD	School based diagnostic categories for consideration by states Guidelines for consideration
Recent Changes	Greater research emphasis Reorganization of some child and DD diagnoses into neurodevelopmental disorders classification Significant changes in Autism Spectrum Disorder diagnostics	ICD-11 in progress No major changes predicted	In revision	Last updated 2004
Professional Focus	Psychiatrists Psychologist	Physician Nurse Practitioners Psychiatrists Psychologists Other Licensed MH Professionals Allied Health Professionals	MH Professionals with IDD expertise	School Professionals and Interdisciplinary teams

Chapter 7 offers recommendations for minimizing the impact of different eligibility criteria across programs.

Fragmented Service Models

Consistent with the expected span of control and responsibility of the education department and local schools, the provision of specialized professional services via school identification and IEP is directly linked to school employed or contracted professionals and provided in coordination with school employees. Within the behavioral health realm, limitations exist on the activities of the professionals, particularly school psychologists. Some of the differences are related to practice and expertise differences and others to employment limitations (Individuals with Disabilities Education Act, 2004; National Association of School Psychologists, 2010) These limits include the following:

1. Focus is primarily on problems within the school environment with minimal to no evaluation of issues across environments.

2. Treatment is designed around the educational activities and goals of the child with minimal to no time devoted to other treatment and support needs in other environments.

3. Treatment and support is directed toward the child with minimal to no supports to the family unit.

4. Qualifications of the professionals are often lower than those for community-based services; for example, school psychologists typically only require a master's degree to independently practice within the school system whereas clinical and consulting psychologists must have a doctoral degree with licensure to practice more broadly in the community. According to the National Association of School Psychologists (2010), over 90% of school districts employ psychologists who only possess a master's degree and thus cannot practice outside of the school setting.

5. There is no requirement to coordinate or collaborate with other treatment professionals in other settings; thus, families and children may see multiple professionals for the same problem with different recommendations from each. This challenge is even more daunting when a child also has an IDD and various professionals and providers in addition to any existing behavioral health needs.

The diagnostic categorizations within the educational system may result in further silos with children assessed as meeting the eligibility criteria on the IDD side not screened for additional behavioral needs and vice versa. This is not prohibitive, but in the author's experience reflects the reality often seen. In reality, individuals whose IDD is clearly apparent often have any additional emotional/behavioral needs overlooked and those with extremely significant behavioral issues may have less common or clear IDD needs missed. The "diagnostic overshadowing" problem begins early in this respect. While the ability of schools to hire professionals with less education and experience may broaden the access to supports within the school setting, the limits on diagnostic expertise and ability to practice outside the school setting could result in missed needs and more fragmented treatment.

Summary

This chapter has focused on the challenges in separation of the educational system from other components of support for individuals with IDD. Some pathways for collaboration do exist. School-based health clinics are often linked to other health related service systems and do offer a mechanism for coordination of needed services accessed via the state's Medicaid program, private insurance, and the educational system (Health Research and Services Administration, 2014). These options point to the viability and need for some coordination. They do not, typically, involve IDD-specific support needs outside the more traditional health and behavioral health services and do not address the needed collaboration across all systems, supports, and settings/situations. Chapter 7 offers recommendations for collaboration with the school system.

Chapter 4

Lost in the Forest:
Which Way Do We Go?

Youth with co-occurring IDD and behavioral health needs minimally navigate two sets of needs/supports and often find themselves engaged with and navigating multiple systems (Brookman et al, 2009; Dorfman & Awmiller, 2003; Jacobstein, Stark, & Laygo, 2007). Understanding and navigating the service system(s) often overwhelms recipients and families (Dorfman & Awmiller, 2003; Jacobstein et al., 2007). For most individuals who receive services and support via state systems, the need to navigate multiple systems is due to no single system containing/funding the full range of supports. Some individuals with IDD will qualify for and receive supports via these available state options; however, for others, particularly youth whose families' financial resources are more substantial, many medical and behavioral health needs may be met via private insurance. These individuals may or may not then qualify for accessing long term supports and services options via state service systems. Availability of Medicare may further add additional systems requiring navigation as does any involvement in other child-related systems such as child and family services or legal involvement with the judicial system. These challenges are evident above the already discussed complication of cross over with the school system. The array of systems an individual with dual diagnosis may encounter include the following:

1. State operated/directed IDD systems (via State funds and/or Medicaid funding)

2. State operated/directed behavioral health systems (via State funds and/or Medicaid funding)

3. State social services programs

4. State juvenile or adult corrections programs

5. State Medicaid health system

6. Medicare federal insurance

7. Private insurance (health and behavioral health)

8. Department of Education and local schools

Navigating these systems becomes even more complicated depending upon the organization of programs within each state system. Typically, corrections and education are not included in the same department/division as disability, health, or behavioral health programs nor are they included together. Thus, minimally an individual and/or family must navigate three different state programs in addition to private insurance and Medicare if the individual purchases/qualifies for these options. Organization of IDD, behavioral health, social services, and Medicaid programs differs greatly from state to state and can either simplify or complicate individual and/or family access. Figure 4a presents organizational variants across states and figure 4b presents the link to early intervention programs.

Figure 4a. Organizational Variants Across States

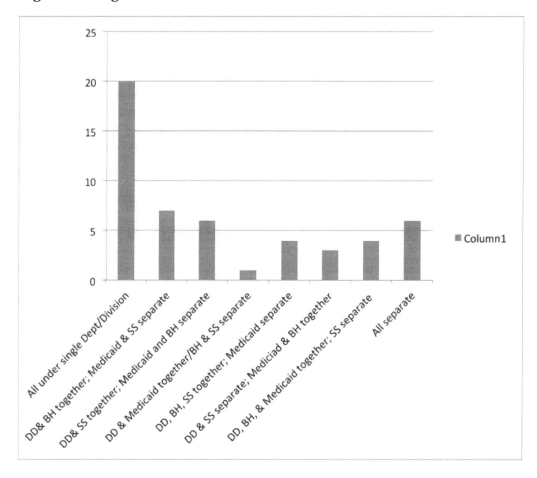

Figure 4b. Early Intervention Organization Across States

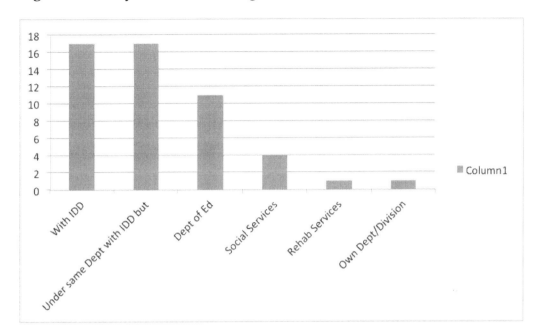

Intellectual and Developmental Disabilities Services

Supports for an individual's IDD surround basic life activities and independence. These supports are most often available via either Medicaid funded options, state initiated programs, or via private pay on the part of the family. IDD support options/programs typically share some key characteristics including:

1. Lifelong supports and a lifespan perspective

2. Focus on supports throughout each person's day as needed to enhance independence

3. Community integration and relationship building

4. Some basic behavioral and environmental approaches when behavioral health issues emerge

5. Interdisciplinary approach across various disciplines (psychology, psychiatry, social work, OT, PT, ST, medical/nursing, dietary, etc.)

Consistent with the support areas noted here, the supports and services typically offered within IDD programs focus on supports to live and work in the community and develop and sustain relationships. Behavioral health supports are not core features of these programs. When present, they focus on the following issues:

1. Professional assessment and support planning

2. Family and staff training to implement behavioral supports

Behavioral Health System Services

Behavioral Health Service are typically implemented with a focus on those with diagnosed mental health conditions creating a system of diagnostic link to services (Emerson, 1995; Jacobstein et al., 2007). These programs are not designed to specifically exclude individuals with IDD, but the needs of individuals with IDD may not be adequately addressed within these programs. Keeping in mind the earlier criteria of consideration of impact of behavioral presentation on determination of need for treatment, a portion of individuals with IDD will not meet typical criteria for receiving behavioral health services. Behavioral health programs tend toward a more psychiatric approach which is more a medical or biologically focused approach of treatment (Moss, 2001; Schuffman & Biagoli, 2014). Services within these programs are more typically consistent with a medical model and are more focused on traditional therapeutic approaches with outpatient and inpatient models available based on assessed intensity of need. Long term or day-to-day supports within these systems may be absent or very limited in nature. Inpatient or out of home treatment options exist for short-term stabilization. Receiving this type of support, even within a crisis, is often a challenge. Siegel and colleagues (2011) identified only nine specialized inpatient programs for youth with IDD and noted there is no clear national strategy to address the needs of these individuals and no focus on adult needs in this area.

Programs and treatment models are most often based in direct patient participation, consent, and a certain degree of communicative ability. Typical options within traditional behavioral health programs include:

- Assessment and diagnostic evaluations
- Outpatient treatment by a licensed mental health professional
- Medication management
- Intermediate more intensive out-of-home options
- Inpatient hospitalization

Specialized evidence-based practice models may be endorsed in some systems with specific criteria and differential payment options. Funding for typical behavioral health services tends to occur via state funding, Medicaid, Medicare, private insurance, or, for some individuals, private pay. As noted in chapter 1, some additional state funding may also occur to support IDD-specific programs.

Autism Spectrum Disorder Services

A newly emerging support option for children focuses on applied behavior analysis most notably as applied in treatment for those with ASDs. As of 2012, thirty-nine states had legislative requirements for private insurance coverage of ASD services for children with 10 also including adults (Cooper, 2013). Recently, states have begun coverage of this service via the Medicaid EPSDT option which opens this intensive option to all children. While this area represents a promising option for individuals and their families, it also may result in additional fragmentation and challenges in coordinating across other support areas.

Medical Services

Medical services typically reflect a range of medically necessary and acute care service needs. Services are typically focused on meeting all medically necessary needs for children and providing for basic medical needs and preventive care for adults. Similar to behavioral health coverage, these services may be accessed via multiple sources including Medicaid, Medicare, or private insurance. Coverage and options may differ across funding options. Typical services available address the following areas:

1. Services for youth (age limits may differ across funding options) which covers a broad array of medically necessary options such as:

   a. Medical services

   b. Dental services

   c. Therapy services (ST, OT, PT)

   d. Home health services

   e. Basic behavioral health services

2. Basic medical services for adults including:

   a. Medical services

   b. Basic behavioral health services

   c. Additional supplemental programs for dental may be available via private insurance or Medicare for some individuals

3. Pharmacy services for youth and adults

4. Emergency room treatment for youth and adults

5. Hospitalizations for youth and adults

Medicare and Interfacing with Medicaid or Supplemental Insurance

Medicare is a federally provided health insurance program for individuals over age 65 and for some individuals under age 65 with specified disabilities meeting certain requirements (Centers for Medicare and Medicaid Services, 2014a). Most individuals with IDD will at some point qualify for Medicare in addition to Medicaid provided all financial requirements are met. At a minimum, dual enrollment will occur with age; however, many may meet either the disability requirements or the dependent child requirement upon enrollment of a parent (Centers for Medicare and Medicaid Services, 2014a). The program differs from Medicaid in several ways. First, unlike Medicaid, no long term support and services can be accessed and paid via the Medicare program. Thus, for individuals with IDD and co-occurring behavioral health issues the day-to-day supports needed must be accessed via other funding options. For health and behavioral health needs, Medicare covers hospitalizations, some home health, hospice, basic outpatient services, some medical equipment, some preventive care services, and medications (Centers for Medicare and Medicaid Services, 2014a). Other health-related services must be accessed via either private insurance, a Medicare gap policy, or Medicaid depending upon each individual's financial situation and choices. For individuals qualifying for Medicare, payment occurs from Medicare as primary and then other noted options for the individual will be assessed.

Challenges in navigating and coordinating across Medicare and Medicaid programs exist and may be further complicated by involvement of other funding sources/programs (Burke & Prindiville, 2011). An initial challenge may surround the differences in funding and operations with Medicare being fully federally funded and operated, while Medicaid represents a federal program implemented and funded in variable ways across states. Additionally, some coverage cross over areas further complicate the situation (Burke & Prindiville, 2011). Medical equipment, medications, skilled nursing and language accessibility services represent areas with coverage across both programs. When coverage exists across systems, coordination of payment and transition across the programs must occur. Lack of communication and data sharing as well as differing standards for eligibility across the programs magnifies these challenges and further complicates an already complex planning and implementation situation (Burke & Prindiville, 2011).

Table 6. Service Options Across Funding Streams

IDD Supports	Behavioral/Mental Health Services	General Medical Services
ADL and IADL supports	Assessment and diagnostic evaluations	Outpatient medical services (including any medically necessary service for children)
Skills and independence training	Individual outpatient therapy	Dental services (for children)
Community Integration Development	Group outpatient therapy	Therapy services (for children)
Vocational training and employment supports	Psychosocial Rehabilitation and Community and psychiatric support	Home Health services
Social skills and relationship supports	Medication management	Pharmacy services
Support to access needed health and behavioral health supports	Intensive residential treatment	Emergency room treatment
	Inpatient treatment	Inpatient medical services

Emerging Trends and Promising Practices

This section has focused on some of the challenges in various systems available for accessing needed services for individuals with IDD and co-occurring behavioral health issues. In spite of these challenges, changes within the healthcare arena present some areas of opportunity as well. Some key emerging trends and promising practices are discussed below.

Managed Care and the Future Face of Supports and Services

Managed care is a familiar concept within the private insurance environment. Because most individuals with IDD will receive a large majority of services via Medicaid and/or Medicare, this recipient population has not been historically exposed to the managed care arena across all support and treatment needs. Within the last decade managed care within the governmental systems has gained traction with more states utilizing managed care options within their Medicaid systems (Barth, Ensslin, & Archibald, 2012; National Council on Disability, 2013).

Inclusion of individuals with IDD has emerged more slowly than that for other populations and has occurred in a variety of ways. Individuals with IDD may receive medical or behavioral health services or both via a Medicaid managed care system. Those who receive both may do so via two separate yet related managed care systems or a combined managed care process. The long term supports and services typically received via the IDD system have not historically been included in Medicaid managed care systems which is not surprising given that managed care originated within the private health insurance arena (National Council on Disability, 2013). More recently, some states are implementing use of managed care methodology within the IDD long term supports and services portion of their systems. While this is a relatively new approach to long term supports and services, it can offer an opportunity for improved coordination across behavioral health, long term IDD services, and any medical needs present for individuals with co-occurring needs. Issues regarding the interface with private insurance for those individuals with private policies, educational programs for youth, and other social service or correctional programs still may challenge navigation and access for individuals and families. The guidelines for improved coordination across systems and programs should still be considered even when a managed care option is implemented.

New Funding Options and Flexibility

In any system we should always keep our eye out for new available funding streams; within the US this has included several new programs that allow states to draw down enhanced federal match dollars tied to improved outcomes for individuals. These include the Balancing Incentive Program, Money Follows the Person, Medicaid waiver options using the 1915i, 1915j, and 1915k applications, and the 1115 demonstration waiver option (Kaiser Commission on Medicaid and the Uninsured, 2009). These new options not only bring potential funding options into the picture but also add a layer of innovation and flexibility not typically seen in existing ICF (institutional) or HCBS options. More information about each of these programs can be found at http://www.medicaid.gov/Medicaid-CHIP-Program-Information/By-Topics/Waivers/Waivers.html.

Summary

This chapter has examined the numerous systems and programs with which recipients and families must interact. The complexity of systems and the new options discussed above must be considered in any strategy to address the complexity of system interactions that exist today. Additional recommendations to address improved coordination will be discussed in Chapter 7.

Chapter 5

Is Anyone Out There?
Finding Help Is Hard!

Most professional training programs lack any inclusion of educational activities geared toward the needs of individuals with intellectual and developmental disabilities. A focus on this area is even more pronounced for professionals aiming to primarily treat adults. Researchers have noted a clear lack of appropriate training programs in North America and Canada (Dorfman & Awmiller, 2003; Schwartz, Ruedrich, & Dunn, 2005; Viecili, MacMullen, Weiss, & Lunsky, 2010). Numerous reports have cited the need for adequate training of health care professionals including reports from the World Health Organization, the United States Surgeon General, the National Institute of Mental Health, and the United Kingdom Department of Health (US Department of Health and Human Services, 2005; US Public Health Services, 2002; Viecili, et al., 2010).

Training and Expertise of Behavioral Health Professionals

The National Association for the Dually Diagnosed (NADD) released a statement in 2013 regarding the needs of individuals with co-occurring IDD and behavioral health needs to be viewed as a "core constituency" within health and behavioral health programs rather than continuing to be viewed as a specialty population. This position has been echoed by the CMS during a joint public policy forum in 2014 (NADD, 2013). However, an overview of research and experience with professionals continues to reveal a basic belief that IDD is and should be treated as a specialty group in behavioral/mental health systems. Healthcare professionals frequently cite a preference not to serve these individuals and indicate that treatment for these individuals should be delivered by specialists. Surveys in recent years have indicated that almost eighty percent of professionals believe specialists must support individuals with IDD and co-occurring mental health needs and have highlighted the lack of appropriately trained clinicians (Jacobstein et al., Smith, 2014; Viecili et al., 2010). Viecili and colleagues (2010) also noted that direct contact with individuals with IDD, coursework focused in the area of IDD and mental health needs, and exposure early in a professional's training can mitigate the comfort and willingness of professionals to provide needed treatment. This finding highlights that exposure and adequate preparation are key factors in building even the smallest degree of comfort in treating individuals with IDD. When reviewing criteria for inclusion in some behavioral health programs and in speaking with various professionals, even those willing to treat individuals with

IDD tend to lose comfort as the degree of disability increases. Most notably, individuals with IDD who have significant challenges in communicating verbally with the treating professionals are more likely to be greeted with denials for services and/or professionals presuming any challenges or presenting problems must be due to the individuals IDD.

From the perspective of the individual and his/her family, the statements noted above can be not only concerning but also somewhat offensive and linked to "rights" issues. A typical response might be: 1) Don't all individuals (with or without IDD) deserve the right to effective behavioral health services? 2) How can a professional, program, or hospital turn someone away solely on the basis of an IQ score or other disability related factor? Yet, it happens every day and in most areas we are not much closer today than we were years ago to addressing this issue. In fairness to the other professionals and program staff, the treatment of individuals with IDD is somewhat more complex than for those without IDD and without exposure, education, and experience most are simply not prepared to offer any meaningful treatment option(s). Additionally, ethics codes for most professional groups require that professionals know and adhere to the boundaries of their competence. Without education, training, and experience, these professionals may feel ethically bound to refer individuals with a dual diagnosis to other professionals.

Let's consider some important unique aspects of providing meaningful and effective treatment for individuals with IDD and behavioral health needs:

1. The typical self-assessment/self-report approach to interviewing and assessment tools will be challenging for some individuals and not possible for others. While IDD can span a variety of conditions and may differ from state to state in terms of conditions warranting additional service eligibility, the most common conditions tend to be intellectual disability and autism spectrum disorders. Individuals with an IDD may experience various challenges in communication that will impact their ability to self-refer, self-report, and respond to questions. Similarly, communication difficulties are a hallmark feature of autism spectrum disorders. With these challenges, professionals accustomed to administering self-report based assessments and conducting clinical interviews may find themselves at a loss in terms of how to assess the situation presented to them.

2. Individuals with IDD often have one or more co-occurring medical conditions in addition to their IDD (May & Kennedy, 2010). For those with a behavioral health condition as well, comorbidity now spans three broad areas: intellectual/developmental disability, medical condition, and behavioral health diagnosis. Determining the interrelationships among these three areas and the symptoms/behaviors associated with each becomes quite complex, particularly when overlaid with the challenges in communication already noted above. In fact, even for individuals without true co-occurring behavioral health diagnoses, medical symptoms paired with communication challenges can result in presentation behaviorally for lack of any other method of communication (May & Kennedy, 2010). Often for those without IDD, professionals within the medical realm will refer for any possible behavioral health concerns and vice

versa. Each professional uses his or her expertise to assess the patient and render any diagnoses and needed treatment. Reports/results will then be shared with the other treating professional. For many individuals with IDD these referrals often result in the individual bouncing between the professionals like a "hot potato" with no one really equipped to assess, diagnose, or treat.

3. Symptom presentation may be somewhat different in individuals with IDD, and the impact of the IDD on the person's functioning must be taken into account in order to determine the additional impact of the behavioral health condition. Significant research has indicated that relying solely on the criteria typically outlined for diagnosis will result in missed diagnoses and that symptoms do exist to point to appropriate diagnoses (Fletcher et al, 2007; Royal College of Psychiatry, 2001). The time, resources, and expertise devoted to the creation of DM-ID and DC-LD are confirmation of these differences.

4. Treatment options often require modifications to achieve efficacy or may differ altogether and support key areas of specific focus and concern as noted below (Charlot & Beasley, 2013; Deb, Clarke, & Unwin, 2006; King et al, 2009; Unwin & Deb, 2008).

    a. Psychotherapy research exists to support modified versions of anger management, dialectical behavior therapy, and cognitive behavior therapy as efficacious for treatment of some behavioral health conditions for individuals with IDD.

    b. Use of techniques consistent with applied behavior analysis are clearly seen as evidence-based practice for several behavioral challenges and some behavioral symptoms associated with diagnosed conditions. Functional behavioral assessments and behaviorally-based treatments may translate into the general child arena but are not as typically used within a general adult population.

    c. Modifications to intensive assertive community treatment options have indicated that individuals with IDD and co-occurring behavioral health needs can be supported using this model with modifications to address flexibility in eligibility, subspecialty training of professionals, and linkages across systems.

    d. There is agreement on best practice approaches to use of medication for people with IDD which are consistent with efforts/focus to reduce reliance on medications and highlight appropriate use. However, they go beyond a diagnostic tie and include other factors.

Knowledge of the factors discussed above is often absent for many clinicians since the assessment and treatment of behavioral health needs for individuals with IDD is not covered in the standard training for these clinicians. Additionally, while most professionals recommend that "specialists" provide the needed assessment and treatment services, specialist training programs are rare.

A Mismatch between Access and Demand

In the introductory chapter of this book, we took a look at general prevalence of co-occurring behavioral health issues for individuals with IDD and noted a significant challenge related to general workforce shortages. Considering the additional information presented at the start of this chapter, the workforce available for individuals with IDD needing behavioral health services is considerably smaller than the inadequate one available to those without IDD (Smith, 2014). The time required to provide successful behavioral health supports to individuals with co-occurring conditions presents an additional variable that sets up a significant demand to access mismatch for these services. The typical approaches of brief therapy or medication management sessions that may work for individuals without IDD will be inadequate for many individuals with IDD. Smith (2014) notes that "superficial involvement" from a "busy" professional is not sufficient to meet the needs of individuals with co-occurring conditions. As noted earlier in this chapter, the general mental health professional work force, which reportedly remains too small to address the needs of the non-IDD population, feels uncomfortable assessing and treating individuals with IDD, and specialist professionals are minimal in number. Thus, the demand for behavioral health services for individuals with IDD is significantly greater than the supply of qualified and willing professionals to meet the needs. Recipients may experience minimal access to specialized services when typical mental health services do not benefit the individual or are denied (Beasley & duPree, 2003).

In the absence of professionals to provide needed focused treatment, many IDD programs/providers find themselves challenged to meet the day-to-day needs of individuals with co-occurring needs. The combined assistance and supports needed by these individuals for both their IDD support areas and their behavioral health needs often results in an over-reliance on staff presence as the solution for these individuals. Often the supports and level of supervision provided far outweigh that needed to address the individual's functional needs. Additionally, the staff relied upon to meet the needs of these individuals are often minimally trained and paid. The typical focus for these staff is assisting individuals with IDD to complete activities across life areas, not addressing complex behavioral health concerns.

Concerning Outcome Trends

In considering the issues in finding an adequate professional work force, it is not surprising that significant negative outcomes occur when adequate access is not available. The importance of adequate identification, treatment, and support for the wide array of behavioral health issues is further underscored by the link between the presence of such issues and negative outcomes. Untreated behavioral health conditions in individuals without IDD can impact a person's ability to have successful relationships, obtain and maintain employment, and take care of many of life's responsibilities. Additionally, because untreated medical conditions may present as behavioral health issues, the underlying medical condition may be left untreated. The continued medical symptoms result in poor health outcomes, hospitalization, and even death. When these challenges are considered within the context of the assistance individuals with IDD need to support communication, interaction, employment, and other life activities, the added potential impact on quality of life (QOL) for individuals with IDD is quite significant.

Removal from activities/community/life

Research indicates that general QOL for those with IDD and behavioral health needs is lower when compared with general population with or without behavioral health conditions (Horovitz, Shear, Mancini, & Pellerito, 2014). Individuals with a dual diagnosis tend to experience fewer relationships, less success at school/work, and less involvement within the local community. In addition to the impact on QOL overall, individuals with co-occurring behavioral health needs represent a high rate of referrals to remaining institutional settings (Braddock et al, 2015; Dorfman & Awmiller, 2003; Lakin et al, 2007). Institutionalization has a negative impact on the individual as well as the system. Obvious impacts relate to loss of community access, independence, and freedom that may solely be due to inadequate behavioral health services rather than legitimate need for out-of-home placement or treatment. As with medical issues, when behavioral health symptoms are left untreated, symptom worsening occurs and may result in institutional living. Within the institutional setting, the individual may learn other challenging responses/behaviors rather than developing more appropriate problem solving and coping strategies. Additional systemic impacts result from the high cost of institutional services. The national trends across states indicate a decrease in the length of stay at institutions. Thus, improvements have been made in trying to re-integrate individuals into a community living option. However, for those leaving the institution QOL ratings may increase slightly but plateau or decrease after the first year (Chowdhury & Benson, 2011). When QOL decreases, individuals may plummet into a cycle of isolation and increasing problems leading to re-institutionalization. Addressing these problems requires a careful look at needed services and supports. A simple change in address or geography will not improve the outlook for these individuals.

Use of High Cost Acute Services

A related area of concern for individuals with IDD and behavioral health needs is rooted in use of the emergency room as behavioral/mental health care when other more appropriate treatment options are not available. When individuals with IDD do not receive needed behavioral health services, crises understandably occur. In the absence of a planned approach to treatment and support for these individuals, the emergency room often acts as the primary doorway to behavioral health services. For those individuals with repeat emergency room visits or for whom a clear danger to self or others is present repeat hospital admissions may occur (Dorfman & Awmiller, 2003). For those for whom acute stabilization of behavioral health symptoms is needed, hospitalization may reflect the most appropriate response. However, for those for whom other variables are at play and/or for whom access to needed preventive and treatment services is a problem, the emergency room visits and hospitalizations are most likely medically unnecessary as well as quite costly. This approach is not only a dead end in terms of appropriate access to needed supports, but also sets up a vicious cycle of repeat visits with misinformed referrals back to the IDD programs including recommendations for institutionalization. The intriguing complication in this cycle is that a person's IDD represents a relatively stable construct. Individuals with IDD tend to learn and grow on a steady trajectory similar to individuals without IDD but on a parallel trend compared to peers without IDD. For the most part IDD symptoms do not wax and wane. Behavioral health symptoms, on the other hand, do often occur in a cyclical pattern with waxing and waning of symptoms occurring. When an individual with IDD and behavioral health needs presents to the emergency room department, the focus can erroneously fall on the IDD. Hospital staff assumes the IDD HCBS provider or institutional options are able to meet the needs and misguided advice and referrals occur due to lack of knowledge about support options and coordination/integration needed.

Summary

This chapter has reviewed the gaps in access to professional services for individuals with a dual diagnosis as well as the factors that likely contribute to the continuation of this access and demand mismatch. Professional knowledge and experience must be addressed to improve access to services. Changes in educational programs must occur as a foundation for the needed improvements in this area. Chapter 8 will provide specific recommendations in this area.

Chapter 6

Get Out the Hammers:
Let's Knock Down the Silo Walls!

As covered in the earlier chapters in this book, navigating complex systems/programs and accessing needed behavioral health supports remains a challenge for individuals with IDD. Most systems/programs rely on what continues to be a small cadre of experts in serving individuals with IDD and behavioral health needs. Building capacity to support these individuals and taking effective practices to scale remains a challenge. We must begin to address some of the big systems challenges and develop effective tools and strategies to knock down the existing barriers.

There are strategies to improve access and quality for individuals with IDD and behavioral health needs. Change and improvement must be approached looking at several key principles.

Person-Centered Approaches

The core of successful treatment and support for individuals with IDD and behavioral health needs must rest within the principles of person-centered thinking and planning that have become the cornerstone of support within IDD systems over the last several decades (Smull, Bourne, & Sanderson, 2010). Person-centered approaches revolve around the following principles:

1. The individual drives/guides his/her own support/treatment

2. Successful planning and support involves the individuals most important to the individual

3. Choice, control, and independence must be central to all activities/approaches

4. A core component must include community involvement

While person-centered approaches are becoming adopted more in traditional health and behavioral health arenas, typical professionals are still able to rely on patient report and prioritization of needs. A thoughtful approach to understanding the goals, desires, and needs of an individual who may communicate and interact differently and rely more on family and other support persons requires more training and different expectations. Thus, for individuals with IDD and behavioral health needs, the formal link to an overall person-centered approach becomes essential. Lack of understanding about negotiables and non-negotiables, preferred people and activities, and life expectations and desires can have a significant impact on behavioral health presentation.

Consistently accepting and cooperating with behavioral health interventions and use of new skills and coping tools requires a certain perseverance not likely to occur unless it is embedded in the broader understanding of goals, desires, and preferences. Setting the stage for success by gaining this understanding can impact motivation and treatment effectiveness resulting in positive outcomes for the individual and his/her family. Typical medical and behavioral/mental health approaches may need to be modified not only in general but to meet the needs of the individual and his/her support system

Programs must also take person-centered approaches to a new level with an infusion of Trauma-Informed Care principles (Keesler, 2014). Trauma-Informed Care is rooted in four key concepts (SAMHSA, 2015):

1. Trauma impacts an individual in significant ways but recovery is possible.

2. Signs and symptoms of trauma should be recognized quickly and early.

3. Trauma principles must be embedded in all responses within a program/organization.

4. Program/organizations must set out to avoid retraumatization.

The importance of Trauma-Informed Care adoption as a normative part of planning and support for individuals with IDD is best understood in the context of the abuse and neglect statistics for individuals with IDD (Hughes et al, 2012a; Hughes et al, 2012b; Sobsey & Doe, 1991; Sobsey, Wells, Lucardie, & Mansell, 1995; Sullivan, 2009; Sullivan & Knutson, 2000).

1. Individuals with disabilities are 4-10 times more likely to be a victim of a crime than individuals without disabilities;

2. Risk of abuse increases by 78% when the individual actually receives services from the disability system; and

3. Risk of abuse is 3.7 times more likely for individuals with disabilities than for those without disabilities.

Person-centered approaches should be adapted in the following ways to include Trauma-Informed practices:

1. Discovery activities should include the addition of specific questions/activities similar to those used in the Adverse Childhood Events (ACE) screen so that support teams identify past trauma, likelihood of ongoing impacts of past trauma, and risk for retraumatization (CDC, 2014).

2. Programs should consider information known from discovery activities related to trauma when using existing tools for staff interviews and "matching" to best support individuals.

3. Plans of support should address the following:

    a. Documentation of known trauma, triggers, and risk to ensure mitigation strategies for retraumatization are in place;

    b. Access of needed supportive therapies and development of coping strategies when appropriate; and

    c. Outline of known cues related to trauma for early identification by family/staff.

4. Families/providers should seek professionals who utilize a Trauma-Informed Care approach when professional assistance/treatment is needed.

5. Monitoring of cues, triggers, and any possible trauma risk should be occurring routinely.

Building on Early Intervention Practices

While changes across life stages often necessitate changes in treatment and support approaches, the developmental needs associated with IDD point to the need to carefully consider the aspects of treatment that may be important to continue even into adulthood. Effective systems for supporting individuals with IDD and behavioral health needs must borrow from the core components of early intervention known to promote sustained and significant improvements. The need for coordination across all professionals remains important for individuals with IDD at any age. The complexities of the developmental, social, medical, and behavioral needs of many individuals with co-occurring needs can only be addressed when coordination is expected, built into the processes, and associated with compensation for the time professionals and providers put into this coordination. A core team of individuals committed to ensuring coordination and implementation of supports must be identified with prioritization of needs across professional areas and in the context of the individual's goals and desires. Lehrer and Ott (2009) demonstrated that use of an interdisciplinary team approach resulted in decreased behavioral challenges, increased community participation, subjective reports of improvements in quality of life, and decreased use of medications for a group of individuals with IDD and challenging behaviors and repeat hospitalizations. Clearly, expanding this approach and highlighting guidelines and expectations is essential to improving outcomes for these individuals with complex needs.

Services must occur within the natural setting as much as possible for the best possible outcomes to be achieved and sustained. This approach means professionals will need to be available within the home, school, work, and community settings. Individuals with IDD will face challenges across most settings and activities given the nature of their disabilities. For those with dual diagnoses, there will be further impacts on many of these life areas along with possible triggers and setting events for behavioral symptoms in some situations. Many of the compensatory and coping strategies that will form the basis of the treatment approaches for these individuals will need to be used across many settings and activities. Individuals will need assistance and/or cues in all of these situations. For those relying on family or staff support, there will need to be modeling and coaching of the family and staff to ensure consistent assistance and cues, as well as to address any potentially contradictory actions that may serve as triggers or setting events.

Building the Right System

Systems/programs must be prepared to move beyond the status quo and implement creative and flexible support packages/options. The changes required will involve review of data and outcomes for individuals with IDD and behavioral/mental health needs. Gaps must be identified with a willingness to look beyond existing solutions. Continuous quality improvement loops must be implemented across IDD and behavioral/mental health indicators to ensure continuous improve and innovation becomes an embedded element in every system/program. This approach will require a move to focus on outcomes over process in reporting. Using this approach, systems/programs must evaluate what's working and what's not. Taking a systematic approach allows for systems to continually ensure the following:

1. What's working remains in the system/program

2. What's not working is stopped

3. New options are implemented to address gaps

Systems/programs must provide for outcomes-based intervention approaches. Barnhill (2006) highlighted the need for a combined biomedical and symptom outcomes data approach for psychiatrists to more responsibly select and monitor medication treatments to maximize symptom improvements and minimize side effects or negative outcomes. Similarly, Pfadt and Wheeler (2006) outlined some key components of a data-based clinical decision making model to ensure treatment objectives are outlined and measured. Despite these types of guidelines, use of data-based decision making in clinical practice remains atypical in this author's experience. Clear guidelines and requirements for interventions should be outlined. Initial treatment selection should be linked to assessment results. Continued approval should be linked to expected and attained outcomes and improvements.

Innovations in Funding and Sustainability

The more that families, providers, and support systems rely *solely* on governmental funding, the less sustainable they may be. While there needs to be a key role within our governmental structure and some funding *must* be committed, there will be limits and there will be ups and downs in national and state fiscal options. The cyclical fiscal climate exists irrespective of political leanings; rather economic ups and downs represent a reality of life (Beasley & duPree, 2003; Thaler et al., 2008). Tying needed supports to governmental funding with no alternative options means more change and lack of continuity for folks. In the same way as many individuals diversify their retirement funding options, diversification of funding streams for supports needed by individuals with disabilities is essential to sustainability of supports over time. Evaluation of possible innovative options reveals a variety of options as a place to begin addressing this concern.

Grant funding can represent a supplemental funding source for governmental entities, university programs, and private provider organizations. Sources of grant opportunities vary across federal grant programs to private foundations. Governmental entities may be eligible for some grant programs and may have opportunities for partnerships with universities for others. Additionally, private providers and professional entities may be eligible. Key factors in many grant opportunities involve creativity and innovation as well as intensity of impact on underserved populations. Programs and/or "research" efforts to explore supports and treatment options for individuals with co-occurring IDD and behavioral/mental health needs could clearly be viewed as perfect proposals for grant funding. Earlier sections of this book focused on the lack of adequate solutions for this population, lack of expertise in providing treatment and support, and the negative outcomes and high costs associated with these failures. The potential improvements in health outcomes and quality of life for individuals along with the potential longer term cost savings to systems would be enticing for any serious grant funding organization including the federal government. For example, the Kansas Department of Aging and Disability Services administers a grant program to provide community-based behavioral health services for children as an alternative to placement in a Psychiatric Residential Treatment Facility (PRTF). This type of program serves to both enhance community-based behavioral health options for individuals with co-occurring needs and to validate possible cost effective alternatives to residential treatment. Programs/providers must invest resources to remain abreast of emerging grant opportunities that may be pertinent to individuals with a dual diagnosis. Exploring these options may infuse additional funding into programs/organizations to allow for continuous quality services and supports. Hiring or contracting with an individual with grant writing experience/expertise should be considered a core resource any organization supporting individuals with dual diagnoses must employ. The benefits of accessing innovative funding opportunities as well as the opportunity to build an organization/program as a model and quality option will more than account for the cost of the added grant writing resource.

In addition to grant opportunities, further innovations in "funding" can be developed via true community networks and partnerships. Opportunities for connections to community networks and associated donations and other fundraising options expand when community connections and partnerships are fostered and considered an essential element for every provider and professional organizations. Suggestions on building community connections and partnerships will be discussed in the next chapter.

Improved Assessment of Needs and Addressing Service Gaps

Typically behavioral and medical treatment is linked to diagnosed and defined symptoms. Similarly, many IDD service systems are beginning to build some sort of formal support needs assessment into the planning process (Agosta, Fortune, Kimmish, Melda, & Smith, 2010). The basis for these processes is typically rooted in one of a small number of assessments designed with a focus on the general needs an individual with IDD has at home, at work and in the community. Some of these assessments may address behavioral needs, but most often from the perspective of the type and amount of support the individual requires from family or staff during a typical day. They do not address the symptom presentation and severity of these issues in any manner that may assist in looking at intensity of behavioral health treatment/supports. Similarly, they do not address the breadth and depth of needed medical supports when an individual also presents with extensive medical needs.

For individuals with multiple presenting needs, assessment approaches must consider the complex interactive effects of these different need sets. Additionally, these interactive patterns may change over time given that medical and behavioral/mental health needs change over time. Each individual may have periods of greater need versus those with much less need. These cyclical patterns are then superimposed upon the generally consistent trend of needs related to an individual's IDD at least until aging concerns emerge. Understanding an individual's level of need and types of supports becomes more complex when these issues are considered together, and grouping of individuals with somewhat similar levels of need in an effort to better predict/determine needed intensity of supports gets more complicated.

An individual's IDD related needs tend to surround assistance and support needed to complete basic activities of daily living and instrumental activities of daily living. Assessment focuses on taking care of oneself, getting ready for the day, working or going to school, accessing and participating in activities in the local community, and developing and maintaining relationships. It may also include a focus on the assistance and support needed to access needed medical/behavioral support and to some degree that needed to implement or comply with recommended medical and behavioral/mental health treatment/strategies when these issues are present.

Behavioral/mental health supports focus more on symptom presentation related to mental health diagnosis or emotional challenges present. Assessments tend to focus on symptoms related to diagnoses, symptom frequency, symptom intensity, and symptom duration. Behavioral health assessments may fall into one or more of several categories.

1. Screening and diagnostic assessments are designed to identify symptoms type and severity (National Council on Behavioral Health, 2011). These tools may be broad based and assist in determining diagnostics or may be diagnosis specific with a focus on measuring treatment progress over time. As discussed in earlier chapters, most screening and diagnostic tools are geared toward those without IDD. IDD specific screening tools do exist to assist a clinician in the differential diagnosis assessment. In either instance these tools are not typically informative in terms of predicting level of need from a supports/treatment

perspective. Individuals with similar diagnostic profiles often present with very different symptoms profiles and may need varied degrees of support/ treatment.

2. Assessments of risk and intensity of need are focused on predicting level and intensity of support needed to prevent and mitigate behavioral health symptoms (Lyons, 2009; Wand, 2012). These tools may be used clinically by treating professionals to measure risk and need or may be used within a service delivery system or program to determine access or eligibility for higher intensity (and often higher cost) services/treatment options. These types of instruments may provide some guidance to clinicians and system assessors of the degree of support needed for a given individual. These tools, like many of the diagnostic tools, are focused on individuals without IDD. Areas of risk and impact focus on some areas that overlap with IDD needs including activities of daily living (ADLs), instrumental activities of daily living (IADLs), work/educational performance, and relationships. However, these tools do not provide a methodology for accounting for the impact of an individual's IDD versus his/her behavioral/mental health needs. IDD specific tools do not exist to address this area. Thus, use of these tools to determine type/intensity of support needed are inadequate for individuals with IDD.

Supports needed may include, but typically go beyond, the help needed from family and staff. Support and treatment options would include professionally delivered therapy in individual or group situations, crisis services, other behavioral supports, and medication prescription and management.

Medical assessments and support needs can add a third layer of issues impacting level of need. However, these types of issues and associated support needs are typically determined based on medical necessity evaluations as determined by medical professionals rather than relying on a specific tool or set of tools.

No single assessment tool or process allows for evaluation of all areas of need across IDD, behavioral/mental health needs, and medical support needs. Nor does a tool or process exist for measuring changes across all IDD, behavioral/ mental health, and medical needs over time. Each individual with co-occurring IDD and behavioral/mental health needs will present with at least two sets of needs likely moving on different yet related trajectories (see Figure 5a). An individual's IDD needs will likely represent a steady increase in skills and independence over time until aging decline begins even though the slope and baseline of the trajectory may be less than that typically seen in same age peers. The individual's behavioral/mental health symptoms and associated challenges will, on the other hand, increase and decrease over time with some periods of basic stability and others of enhanced symptom presentation and problems across life areas. If the individual also presents with significant medical diagnoses and symptoms, a third layer of increasing and decreasing symptoms will also be superimposed on top of the fairly steady IDD and cyclical behavioral/mental health symptom presentations (see Figure 5b).

Figure 5a. Behavioral Health and IDD Developmental/Lifespan Trajectories

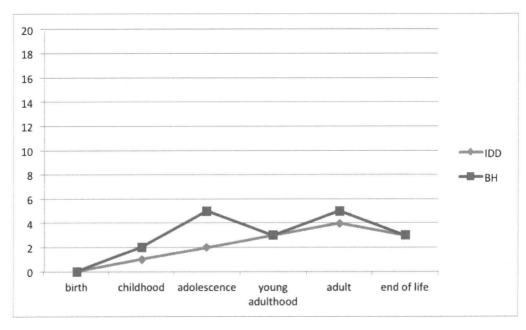

Figure 5b. Behavioral Health, IDD and Medical Lifespan Trajectories

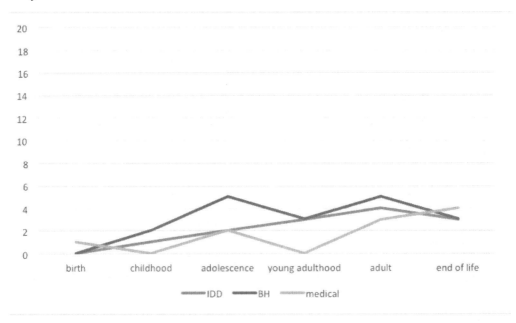

At any given point and time, the individual may present with the various symptom combinations across these three areas. Figure 5 illustrates the basic interplay across symptom areas. IDD needs typically exist within high, moderate, or low areas of need which are fairly consistent across one's life. Some exceptions may exist for specific genetic conditions; however, for these conditions a known profile of changes in need can be expected and adjustments made as needed. Because needs in this arena do not change frequently, assessment of support needs may not need to occur at frequent intervals. As noted previously, behavioral/mental health and medical needs may increase and decrease over time. These areas may require more frequent assessment and may appear to further impact the basic IDD functional areas. For example, an individual with relatively low levels of support need related to his/her IDD may have more difficulty completing basic daily tasks if he/she is depressed, anxious, or psychotic. This increased need for supports will remit if the behavioral/mental health symptoms are treated and subside. Similar types of patterns can occur with medical needs, and interplay between medical and behavioral health issues can complicate the picture. For example, an individual with significant aggression related to psychosis may display additional aggression due to significant pain related to a medical condition. Thoughtful and comprehensive assessment approaches are needed to tease out each factor impacting the presentation which then leads to important treatment components.

Figure 6. Level of Need

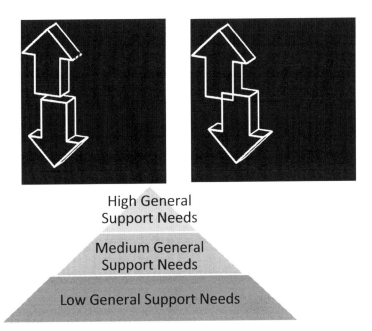

Foundational assessment of each individual's level of support need related to his/her IDD should occur at routine intervals with at least annual review. Full reassessments are likely not needed annually so long as a review is undertaken to allow for identification of any changes in status that may be unanticipated. Individuals with co-occurring behavioral/mental health needs will need assessment more frequently, although specific intervals of assessment will vary depending upon the severity and stability of presenting symptoms. An individual with a fairly stable diagnosis and symptom pattern may only require an annual assessment of risk and support intensity need. Individuals with a more unstable pattern of symptom presentation or those in the midst of an episode of increased symptoms may require more frequent assessments. Frequency may vary depending upon condition and presentation and may range from daily during a period of extreme instability such as during inpatient hospitalization to quarterly for individuals with known cyclical patterns but not currently actively displaying symptoms. Medical evaluations may vary similarly depending upon symptom presentation, profile and stability.

Considering the challenges of assessing level of need, it may raise questions related to the necessity of getting to the bottom of these various symptom profiles. However, the importance of obtaining as accurate as possible a picture of each individual's level of need across areas and across time cannot be ignored. Various funding mechanism and programs set eligibility tied to identified challenges and needs. Providers and service systems may need to adjust typically accepted ideas of support and treatment options along with creativity and flexibility within and across options. Planning must support identification of possible crisis situations and risks, strategies to prevent and mitigate them and interventions should they occur. Varying intensity and type of support may be needed at different times.

Summary

Just as in individual support planning, any effective system/program plan of action must begin with non-negotiables. This chapter has reviewed the key non-negotiables to begin developing innovations in dual diagnosis:

1. Systems/programs must embed person-centered approaches within all policies/procedures/practices.

    a. Expectations for all staff, executives, and consultants/partners to the system/program must be outlined.

    b. Person-centered approaches must be taken to the next level with integration of Trauma Informed Care principles

    These efforts form the foundation of all other activities and are essential to successful outcomes for individuals with a dual diagnosis.

2. Expansion and definition of the "team" must be addressed. Specific ideas about coordination across professionals and facilitation of team activities will be further discussed in Chapter 7, while Chapter 8 will address improved professional expectations and training.

3. Incorporation of naturalistic supports and tips and tools for supporting families and other support staff is essential. Expectations for in vivo supports must be included in all system/program requirements and sustainability efforts must be implemented to incentivize and support this approach. Chapter 9 will further address specific recommendations for family and staff support and training.

4. Systems/programs must invest resources to develop funding diversity. This approach may begin with grants and other supplemental funding exploration and continues with community partnerships and options for fund raising/volunteering/donations. Further discussion of community networks and partnerships will occur in Chapter 7.

5. Improved understanding and expectations for comprehensive assessment and level of need determination must be outlined and cover not only IDD day-to-day supports, but also changing and cyclical behavioral and health needs.

These foundational principles set the stage for an improved approach and for the implementation of some of the more specific recommendations in the following chapters.

Chapter 7

Who's on First?:
Improving Teamwork and Coordination Across
Professionals within the System(s)

Effectively supporting individuals with co-occurring IDD and behavioral health needs must be embedded in a foundation of a coordinated and integrated planning and support structure. The key to making this sort of process successful rests in clear expectations and support for cross professional activities embedded in a broader support team process heavily focused on each individual's vision and goals. For coordination to occur as needed, we must build systems that allow for seamless access across specialty areas at least from the consumer perspective. Most medical and behavioral health systems rely to a large degree on the patient to coordinate across his/her various professionals and to report issues either verbally or by bringing test results or other documents from professional to professional. In managed care systems, there is a broad level of coordination for those with high use of services or with complex medical or behavioral health needs which, where available, many of these individuals would qualify to receive. Even when this coordination is available, it does not address the integration with other important life issues that individuals with IDD may be challenged to do on their own.

A first step in improving coordination lies in development of a truly integrated plan of care/support. To accomplish this level of integration, professionals must communicate beyond the basics of sharing each individual assessment and plan. There must be a collaborative effort to discuss the various aspects of the individual's needs across areas. Assessment and balancing of risk issues across professional areas, and further consideration of the balance of all of the "important for" recommendations from the professionals with the "important to" issues from the person's perspective is essential (Smull et al., 2010). Most individuals without IDD do this sort of "balancing" on their own. With information from any health or behavioral health professional, these individuals will consider the current symptoms they experience, the risks of the symptom continuation, the proposed treatment approach, the benefits and risks of the proposed treatment, and how both the symptoms and proposed treatment relate to the other important things in their life. Following this "evaluation" the person then determines if he/she will pursue treatment and if so which treatment option seems best for him/her. Individuals with IDD and co-occurring behavioral health issues often need assistance in this sort of evaluation, thus requiring a level of engagement from the professionals involved beyond the typical symptoms and treatment parameters most professionals may be accustomed to providing.

To accomplish the level of assessment and planning described above, systems must contain mechanisms for coordination time so that all involved professionals and the individual's support system can understand the complexity of needs and impact of one treatment approach on another. Examples of crossover issues between professional areas are discussed in Table 7:

Table 7. Cross Discipline Coordination Examples

PT gait issues and independence:

1. Professional recommendations

   PT recommendation – Gait belt to address unsteady gait and prevent falls

   Behavioral Health recommendation – Increased freedom of movement to address anxiety

2. Team considerations

   High risk of falls and history of falls – use of gait belt with planned exercise and walks

   Low to moderate risk and no history of falls – no use of gait belt

   Low to moderate risk and history of falls – modified plan for use of gait belt in higher risk situations

---

Obesity concerns and need for control in borderline personality disorder:

1. Professional recommendations

   Medical recommendation – prescribed diet

   Behavioral health recommendation – choice in meals and snacks to minimize power struggles

2. Team considerations

   High medical risk with injury or mortality probable – team works to construct diet and ensure compliance

   Moderate medical risk and no injury or mortality likely – modified diet with compliance focused on most necessary issues/food items and choice in other areas

   Low medical risk – No prescribed diet; team works to build support plan to improve healthy decisions based in person-centered discovery framework

---

Neurology and psychiatry medication management:

1. Professional recommendation

   Neurology recommendation – decrease Antiepileptic Drug to simplify medication regimen

   Psychiatry recommendation – maintain Antiepileptic Drug to continue to augment mood stabilization

2. Team considerations

   Team must coordinate neurology-psychiatry joint consultation to determine best course of action weighing both seizure and mood symptoms while balancing medication simplification goal

---

Medication side effects presenting as behavioral challenges:

1. Presenting issue

   Individual presents with irritability and increased aggression

   New antipsychotic recently initiated

2. Team considerations

   Presentation of data to psychiatrist for consideration of different medication to treat MH symptoms and perhaps resolve akathisia

   Titrate medication down to minimize side effects but maintain efficacy

---

Facilitation and Coordination of Supports/Treatment

IDD service options inherently surround some form of support coordination or case management. As noted in Chapter 3, HCBS options contain a requirement for case management and ICF/IDD providers must provide a support plan coordinator. This case management/coordination function involves facilitation of a required support team. However, composition of the team occurs on an individual basis with the only mandatory participants being the individual, support coordinator/case manager, and representatives from any direct residential or day-to-day staff support system. Inclusion of other involved professionals is encouraged but not required. Additionally, as noted previously, individuals may encounter case managers/care coordinators within their health and behavioral health programs via private insurance or Medicaid.

Enhanced expectations and requirements must be introduced to address the needs of individuals with a dual diagnosis. To achieve enhancements in facilitation and coordination and achieve adequate planning and support, educational and certification programs must become the norm for anyone in a role of coordinating or facilitating supports and treatment for individuals with a dual diagnosis which may include the IDD support coordinator, behavioral health coordinators, or nurse/medical case managers. Recommended options for consideration in this area include:

1. University programs should consider bachelor's level case management specialization in IDD. States should consider partnering with key public universities to design and offer specialization within their psychology or social work undergraduate programs. These undergraduate areas of study represent professions that often require post graduate study which many students will not obtain. While those who go on to complete graduate training represent those who may go on to provide professional behavioral health services, those who do not could, with some training, fill a significant gap in current systems and offer a career path for these students.

2. Providers and systems should consider requiring and/or accepting specialized certification and credentialing programs with tie in to pay incentives or supervisory advancement options. State IDD staff and provider organizations could also consider partnering to develop state-specific credentialing and certification programs. These programs could represent an additional option for support coordination/case manager trainees without existing specialized training or a required state option designed to specifically align with the state's system requirements and service options.

3. Systems/programs (regardless of funding mechanism) should identify required training for all key staff involved in coordinating and facilitating support for those with a dual diagnosis. Minimally, training and education should be required in the following:

   a. Positive Behavior Supports and integration with person centered planning/thinking approaches

   b. Facilitation and communication across professionals

c. Recognizing signs of behavioral health issues

d. Recognizing signs and symptoms of medical issues and relationship to presenting behavioral challenges

Improved Cross Specialty Coordination

Given that individuals with IDD and behavioral health needs often present with complex support need profiles, cross specialty coordination becomes essential. Supports related to the individual's IDD may be needed in the home, at work/school, and in the community to support involvement and independence. Behavioral health supports may be needed and involve professional level supports as well as caregiver-provided supports within all life settings. Additionally, comorbid medical conditions may also be present necessitating medical and allied health supports.

Integration with the school system

Coordination of supports must include the school system and involves both teachers and professionals practicing within the school system. Supports initiated within the school system should form the foundation for supports during the educational years. System collaboration should include investigation of opportunities for reducing duplication and improving coordination.

For individuals with IDD and behavioral/mental health needs, school changes must begin at the diagnostic and eligibility phases. Similar to approaches being implemented within the Medicaid Balancing Incentive Program, school special education processes should include at least a screening process that ensures that assessment does not stop once eligibility for at least some set of support options is met. That is, a child with very significant IDD needs may also meet requirements for emotional/ behavioral support needs and should be assessed for dual eligibility with the results informing a comprehensive individual education plan encompassing both IDD and behavioral/mental health needs. The same should occur for a child who may have fewer support needs related to his/her IDD but very significant emotional/behavioral needs. While this type of thorough evaluation of needs across areas may occur within some school systems, it is not routinely completed nor is it required.

Past the eligibility process, support approaches for youth must also be integrated and coordinated. A basic approach to improved coordination and minimization of duplicate or contradictory supports could involve required cross system assessments and plans. In this type of system, an over-arching team with members from both the educational and IDD and/or behavioral health systems would plan and complete joint or complementary assessments and work together to develop a support plan with complementary strategies across the school and home settings. Parents would have an opportunity to work collectively with all professionals involved in their child's support and treatment and could explore similarities and differences across settings and situations. Maximizing the benefits of the already existing and required school-based assessments and information could help to determine in a more appropriate manner when and what type of complementary supports are needed outside of the educational setting.

Integration and coordination could be taken a step further by diving slightly deeper than required integration and coordination. For individuals accessing services from multiple state programs, cross program coordination could include determination of primary or lead responsibilities based upon age and symptom profile. Recommendations for this approach can be seen in Table 8. Implementation of a more systematic coordination of supports offers the best opportunity for consistency and sustainability of options available for individuals with co-occurring needs. Private insurance companies should also consider supporting and funding needed collaborative activities not traditionally reimbursed and perhaps not typically considered "healthcare" activities. Consistency across life situations and supports whether that is at home, in the community, in a healthcare environment, or at school is essential to improved health and behavioral health outcomes for individuals with IDD. Missteps in a single arena or by some support area can have substantial impact on behavioral health symptoms/presentation and lead to avoidable and costly treatments or hospitalizations. Private insurers should use the same guide provided here to determine how they may best work with school and public programs.

Table 8. School Integration and Coordination

Support Profile	School System	IDD System	Behavioral/ Mental Health System	Medical System
Moderate IDD Minor aggression at school and home No significant medical issue	Lead role Professionals assess; recommend learning/behavioral interventions Consultation to other systems to implement needed supports	Provides in home support options Staff follow school plan in the home with modifications Family/provider share data with school	May have no significant role unless child also has medication need	Basic preventive medical services
Significant IDD Severe Self-injury with co-occurring diagnosis GI symptoms	Focused on educational needs Professionals consult with IDD experts; incorporate recommendations into school IEP Monitor of GI irregularities and reporting to MD; modified mealtime supports	Lead role IDD clinicians provide assessment and intervention recommendations Consultation to other systems to implement supports Oversee all in home supports; Monitor of GI irregularities and reporting to MD	Provide any needed medication management Joint consultation and assessment with IDD experts to access any needed BH services	All needed medical services Consultation with IDD experts to determine best balance of dietary needs Consultation with school personnel on needed supports and monitoring
Mild IDD Major Depression Diagnosis Weight issues	Focused on educational needs Professionals consult with BH & MD; incorporate recommendations into school IEP	Provides in home support options Staff follow BH recs in POC Family/provider share data with school; BH & MD	Lead role Assessment and Treatment recommendations provided Consultation with others to implement	Coordinate with BH professional with staff and family input to balance diet needs

Medical Home Models and Innovation

The medical or health home model results in significant improvement in health outcomes for individuals with significant/chronic health conditions and represents an innovative option highlighted in the new Affordable Care Act (Affordable Care Act, 2010; Centers for Medicare and Medicaid Services, 2014c; Kastner, & Walsh, 2012). The model involves a more centralized, one stop version of providing medical care and is designed to enhance coordination across professionals. Recent efforts across the nation have looked at implementation and outcomes of this type of model for individuals with IDD. Improvements have been noted with the medical home model and people with IDD or ASD and behavioral health needs (Charlot, 2014). Outcomes have included increased satisfaction, decreased behavioral challenges, decreased use of emergency room services, decreased hospitalizations, maintenance of home environment, and treatment of preventable but previously unidentified health problems. At a minimum, health home models must include primary care services, specialists typically accessed for individuals with IDD, allied health professionals, and behavioral health clinicians to achieve the level of health integration needed for individuals with IDD and co-occurring behavioral health needs to improve their health outcomes.

To maximize positive outcomes for individuals with a dual diagnosis, the health home model has in some states been modified to place the primary IDD provider at the core rather than the individual's primary care physician (Spotts, 2012). This model places the point of coordination where it appropriately rests with the provider responsible for day-to-day supports. Given that for these individuals integration is necessary across professionals involved and the staff and family supporting the person each day, the greatest likelihood of success occurs when the provider recruiting and monitoring staff supports also develops relationships and assists with coordination across professionals.

Figure 7. IDD Behavioral Health Home Expansion Model

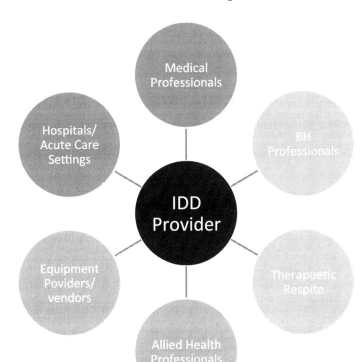

A further extension of this approach would present an even greater opportunity for success in supporting these individuals. The base of any well developed and implemented behavioral health strategy must continue to rest in the person-centered and thinking processes espoused within all IDD programs and now included in actual federal regulations for home and community based supports (Centers for Medicare and Medicaid Services, 2014b). With this in mind, the health home model could be expanded further to a community support model. The movement of the primary IDD provider to the center of the model of support would remain with the understanding that the provider does not usurp either the recipient's role in driving their supports or the role of the family and other naturally occurring supports in the recipient's life. Rather, the model is addressing the core coordinated and linked supports surrounding the person. The primary IDD provider's role is to play a facilitative role in ensuring the individual is able to access all needed supports related to health and safety as well as general life and relationship supports. Each primary provider develops an array of relationships in relevant groups and areas. Health and behavioral health professionals or organizations would represent a part of this array. This model would then go beyond the basic health home approach and broaden to include community, educational, and vocational organizations. The purpose of this extension would center on several key elements variably implemented in current systems. Links to these types of groups would pave the way for supporting individuals to develop an array of connections across their community and consistent with their interests/preferences. Similarly, the individuals would gain increased opportunities to learn new skills, build new relationships, and ultimately increase their independence. A secondary benefit would be the opportunity to tap into community and faith based support connections that may draw from different and new funding streams and possible volunteer programs, expanding the options for the individual's supports and the sustainability of those supports. Families and other naturally occurring supports would be nurtured and supported in their roles within the individual's life.

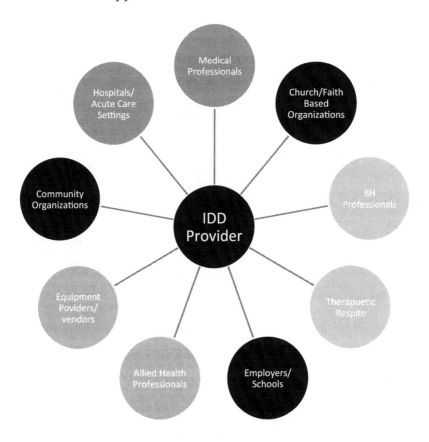

Figure 8. IDD Behavioral Health Home Expansion Plus Provider-Community Partnerships

Improved Triage and Transition Planning

Given the complexity of needs for individuals with a dual diagnosis paired with the already heavy use of emergency rooms and hospitals, it is reasonable to presume that hospitals will continue to be (at least for some time) a significant location for encounters between professionals and individuals with IDD and behavioral health needs. As discussed in earlier chapters, the experience of professionals within hospital and emergency room settings does not typically include any specialized training in supporting and treating these individuals. When individuals present to the hospital for treatment, a crisis of some sort is being experienced within the individual's support system irrespective of the causal factors. The individual and his/her support network are in significant need of immediate assistance. The type of assistance may be varied, but the need for professional assistance in assessing the situation or presenting problem and offering guidance and direction as well as treatment where needed is clear. Otherwise, the presentation to these settings would not occur.

Development of hospital triage programs may offer an important opportunity to both positively impact the health and QOL outcomes for individuals and the knowledge and comfort of professionals in providing services to them. Partnerships via the state, UCEDD or other IDD organization, and local hospitals offers the opportunity to use expertise within specific state programs/organizations to build the capacity of the staff and professionals within the hospital to appropriately assess, treat, and/or direct individuals and their families and providers.

A pathway to develop a hospital triage system would involve the following activities:

1. Key local hospitals should be identified based upon available data regarding emergency room visits and hospital stays.

a. Major regional and urban areas should be covered.

b. Initial focus should balance adequate coverage with professional capacity to meet each hospital's need.

2. The state/UCEDD/IDD organization would establish identified clinician liaisons with community hospital triage programs

3. Clinician to clinician activities should include at a minimum the following:

   a. Modified on-call process wherein the clinician liaison is contacted and made available within set parameters of defined urgency to triage existing cases with hospital staff. This would likely not involved a true 24 hour on-call access as hospital treating physicians would be expected to complete these activities. Rather the focus is on consultation within a quick period of time to treating physicians for difficult/stuck cases.

   b. Regular case review activities should be implemented at set intervals to address known areas of concern including diagnostics, treatment options and appropriate medication approaches, and support and transition planning.

   c. In hospital consultation and assistance in recommended treatment and modification to approaches should occur for individuals admitted.

   d. The clinician liaison would connect hospital staff with appropriate points of access within existing systems to facilitate locating and preparing additional needed community professional supports.

   e. Hospital staff training and mentoring would occur throughout all processes with a heavy focus on in vivo opportunities as each individual situation is triaged.

4. Outcome indicators should be identified and monitored to determine success and remaining gaps. Reviews with involved state/UCEDD/IDD organization staff and clinicians as well as hospital staff and professionals to determine effective components of the program and needed modifications should occur routinely.

Implementation of programs as defined above would allow states to take what may presently be a small number of experts and systematically use their experience and knowledge to positively impact the system in key moments of crisis when missteps are most costly. This approach also offers a mechanism for training on the job for professionals who might otherwise not avail themselves of more traditional types of training that require time away from work with no pay or worse additional costs.

For individuals admitted to the hospital or other institutional or residential program, consistent transition planning processes and expectations must be in place. Many states have implemented detailed processes for transition from public institutions consistent with expectations in federal requirements in Olmstead v. L.C. (1999) (Perez, 2012). The lessons learned in development and implementation of these processes should be translated across institutional settings to ensure that discharge planning begins at admission when a clear focus on reason for treatment/admission can be articulated and discussed and can guide treatment and discharge decisions. As time passes, particularly for stressed and burned out support systems, the respite offered by the admission can negatively impact readiness for bringing the individual home, and treatment teams within the institutional settings can begin to veer into new and different areas of support and treatment that do not necessitate remaining out of the home. Beginning the discussion at admission ensures the issues most impacting support at home are identified, and assessment and treatment can proceed in an orderly fashion. Modifications to approaches occur only based on clear assessment information and in a well thought out and discussed manner using data and information within a team process.

To implement a hospital and institutional transition process, states/programs should include the following:

1. Begin with any established Olmstead transition processes already in existence within the state.

2. Identify modifications for particular settings/situations such as medical assessments of hospitalization status as initial basis of discharge from the hospital rather than required interdisciplinary focus within a typical ICF/DD or situations in which an individual's preference comes into play and those such as hospitals where they do not.

3. Set expectations for all participating hospitals and institutions related to discharge planning and required transition activities to ensure that infor-

mation learned during hospital or institutional stay are translated appropriately to community/home settings to ensure positive health outcomes and reduce the likelihood of hospital or institutional admission in the future.

4. Dedicate/obtain IDD expert resources to facilitate and assist transition planning.

Implementing consistent expectations for discharge and transition planning maximizes the ability to support individuals in their homes and minimizes any form of out of home treatment or support. Facilitation and oversight by identified staff and clinical resources can also ensure that individuals do not move from one institutional setting to another due to failure to carryover needed supports to the home setting. Similar to triage options, identification and monitoring of key identified outcome indicators can assure success via support for effective system components and requirements as well as identification of and planning to address continued gaps in services.

These options can occur via state initiated efforts, UCEDD initiated efforts, or other provider driven initiatives. Grant funding may also be available to support such efforts.

Partnerships and Collaboration

In addition to the systematic and paid resources and "team" players discussed in the earlier sections of this chapter, partnerships and collaborative opportunities with community organizations must become an integral part of each system. If the ultimate outcome of each support plan is individually defined community lives for people with IDD and behavioral health issues then we must bring the community into the picture. Without greater effort in this area, individuals with a dual diagnosis will continue as Smull and colleagues (2010) note to simply lead "good but paid lives." Lives that are more focused on day-to-day things that matter to the person and his/her preferences but that are heavily dependent upon people paid to assist them and spend time with them. This challenge exists even for those without a dual diagnosis; thus, if the institutional data discussed earlier is considered, it is not difficult to see that those with more complex needs are even more likely to struggle to build community connections and relationships. Several areas warrant focus from IDD programs:

1. Partnerships between state IDD systems and private providers should be explored to develop innovative programs aimed at filling known system gaps. Examples may include the following:

   a. For states with state-funded behavioral health programs or expertise, the state IDD agency and private providers could partner to offer programs aimed at specialized services to address dual diagnosis needs. This approach would result in shared responsibility for and funding of these specialized programs.

    b.   State programs could offer grant opportunity to address specific gaps that are identified. Private provider applications could be solicited with funding aimed at those with the best proposal to address the described gap and includes a solid outline of outcome expectations and measurements. These types of grant approaches could be fully state funded with outlined flexibility or a component of a state application for federal grant options.

2.   Existing IDD providers must reach out to local community organizations (volunteers, church groups, community groups, etc.) to develop local resource teams and partnerships to more effectively collaborate to support individuals with complex needs.

3.   Building community networks and connections must become an integral part of planning for each individual. Planning must include active efforts to get others involved and to connect individuals to organizations. Outreach by state agencies and/or providers must occur to identify interested and committed groups (organizations or people) to begin this process.

4.   University partnerships must be created to provide support for professional training and grant options for pilot projects and applied systemic research.

These efforts should be part of planning within the IDD system as well as individual programs. Provider evaluations (in any system) should consider their involvement in these efforts both upon request from the state/funder and upon provider initiative.

Summary

This chapter has addressed one of the most challenging yet most important aspects of breaking down silos for individuals with a dual diagnosis: collaboration and coordination. Several key areas and recommendations in each area were covered including improvements in facilitation and coordination of a team, integration across school, home and other health areas, innovative approaches to and use of the medical home model, coordination across acute and non-acute supports, and other community networks and partnerships. Each system/program supporting individuals with IDD must consider all of the recommended issues and evaluate internally which apply to their system/program. Without improvements in these noted areas, fragmentation of supports will continue to impact negatively individual outcomes and to strain the resources of any system/program.

While involvement or leadership may occur via state or federal entities, the activities outlined here may be carried out or initiated by other programs/providers or university affiliated groups. In fact, leadership at the local or provider level will most likely result in real partnerships with sustainable change that works for and meets the needs of individuals in that area. Support from and coordination with the state and federal entities involved in services can then serve to enhance the outcomes.

Chapter 8

Navigating Future Storms: Building the Next Generation of Professionals and Leaders

An essential area of focus and development to improve outcomes for individuals with IDD and behavioral health needs must center on building the professional provider base to support and treat these individuals. Given the lack of adequate access to needed behavioral health services in general along with the previously noted beliefs in need for specialized training and practice for individuals with co-occurring needs, other strategies aimed at increasing access and outcomes cannot succeed without addressing this clear gap in the current systems nationally. Munir (2009) noted that training and education of professionals is "unplanned" and lacks even a basic exposure to the needs of individuals with co-occurring conditions. Successfully impacting this area requires a two-pronged approach: 1) focus on long term strategy to attract and train young up and coming professionals and 2) outreach, mentoring, and training for existing professionals to address current needs.

Required Training and Experience

An effective strategy to address the noted NADD and CMS recommendation that individuals with a dual diagnosis must be considered a "core constituency" rather than a specialty behavioral health group will require an approach likely similar to that taken in many health fields. General knowledge and practice expectations must be set and integrated into all training programs across behavioral health disciplines, while specialty training may be needed for treating complex presentations particularly when individuals present with needs across IDD, behavioral health, and medical realms.

To achieve this goal, the general professional providers within the behavioral health arena must be trained to understand and apply basic principles of support and treatment for individuals with IDD and behavioral health needs, Specialty behavioral health training programs or program components could then be offered to those interested in practicing within this area as a significant portion or in total for their practice. Each university program aimed at training behavioral health professionals should build into each program basic exposure, knowledge, and experiential opportunities for all students.

Basic exposure and knowledge must address at a minimum the following areas:

1. Prevalence of behavioral health needs for individuals with IDD
   a. Co-occurring mental health diagnoses
   b. Behavioral issues associated with medical conditions
   c. Genetic conditions and behavioral phenotypes
   d. Other behavioral challenges and needs
2. Impact of IDD presentation on assessment and diagnostic practices
   a. Developmental considerations
   b. Communication challenges and assessment modifications
   c. Introduction to diagnostic modifications and considerations
3. Impact of IDD presentation on treatment approaches and modifications
   a. Developmental considerations
   b. Positive Behavior Supports and involvement of family and staff
   c. Modified therapeutic approaches

Coverage of these basic areas could be addressed via a required IDD and behavioral health introductory course, via inclusion of IDD modules within existing courses, or by a combination of these two approaches. In addition to the basic exposure and knowledge that may be accomplished within coursework activities, each behavioral health professional in training should obtain at least a minimal level of practicum or clinical experiences involving individuals with IDD and behavioral health needs. Similar to the course work options, these practicum experiences may be accomplished through IDD specific rotations within practicum options and/or ensuring that practicum experiences occur with providers/organizations who as a matter of practice support/treat individuals with co-occurring needs within a more general practice approach. Increasing basic knowledge and comfort would allow for general professionals to meet the needs of those with more minimal behavioral health issues and identify and make appropriate referrals for those with more significant needs.

IDD and Behavioral Health Specialty Graduate Training

Only a handful of university programs have established and recognized specialty training in IDD and behavioral health issues for their graduate behavioral health programs such as psychiatry, psychology, and social work degree programs. In considering the challenges in supporting individuals with co-occurring needs, specialized training programs must be developed and implemented. Examples of specifically designed IDD specialized programs that may serve as models for consideration include the IDD Psychology program at Ohio State University and the Psychology training program through the JFK Developmental Disability Center at the University of Colorado (Regents of the University of Colorado, 2014; The Ohio State University Nisonger Center, 2014). Each of these programs offer varied methods for specialty learning and training in treating individuals with IDD and behavioral health needs; however, both of them emphasize some coverage within existing coursework as well as specifically designed practicum/clinical activities. Many professionals in the field today have built careers in research and treatment following training and mentoring by another dedicated professional through their graduate program, internship or other post-doctoral training. However, these training experiences are dependent upon the presence of the specific mentor rather than based within a formally designed IDD specialization within a behavioral health training program. The two programs noted here are examples of well documented and designed training programs specific to this area of specialization with existing and consistent teams of clinicians devoted to classroom, research and practica experiences. Both of these programs are also associated with the state University Center of Excellence in Developmental Disabilities (UCEDD). A similar program also exists for psychiatry residents in Ohio (Ruedrich, Dunn, Schwartz, & Nordgreen, 2007; Schwartz et al., 2005). Essential components of any specialized training program should include the following:

1. Required didactic classroom training

    a. Comprehensive introduction to IDD

        i. Overview of IDD and differences across states/systems

        ii. Genetic conditions associated with IDD and associated behavioral phenotypes

        iii. Medical complexities commonly associated with IDD

        iv. Long term support needs for individuals with IDD

        v. Prevalence of behavioral health needs in individuals with IDD

        vi. Person centered thinking and practices in behavioral health and IDD

    b. Assessment and diagnosis of behavioral health conditions for individuals with IDD

        i. Assessment guidelines and key considerations

        ii. Diagnostic modifications and differences to include in depth coverage of the DM-ID and DC-LD

        iii. Common comorbidities

        iv. Considering behavioral phenotypes and impact

        v. Identification of behavioral health needs in the absence of clear diagnosis

        vi. Modified assessment tools and IDD specific assessment tools

    c. Evidenced based practice in IDD and behavioral health to include at a minimum

      i.   General treatment approaches for supporting individuals with IDD and behavioral health needs

      ii. Applied Behavior Analysis and Positive Behavioral Support approaches/methodology

      iii. Cognitive Behavioral Therapy and modified approaches

      iv. Dialectical Behavioral Therapy and modified approaches

      v.   Emerging practices

      vi. Monitoring of treatment efficacy

  d. Psychopharmacology and IDD

      i.   Prescribing guidelines for practitioners

      ii. Idiosyncratic responses to medications

      iii. Medication side effects and impact on behavioral challenges

      iv. Monitoring of treatment efficacy

      v.   Interactions with other medications for medical needs

  e. Specialized education in autism spectrum disorders

      i.   Prevalence

      ii. Assessment and diagnosis

      iii. Common comorbidities

      iv. Specialized treatment approaches

2. IDD specific practicum/clinical activities to include exposure to and training in the following

  a. Assessment and diagnosis of IDD and ASD

  b. Assessment and diagnosis of co-occurring behavioral health needs

  c. Interdisciplinary approaches and interactions

  d. Treatment approaches appropriate for discipline which may include

      i.   Applied Behavioral Analysis and Positive Behavior Supports approaches

      ii. Individual and group therapy

      iii. Psychopharmacology and medication management

3. IDD specific internship to include additional formal opportunities similar to those outlined in practicum area with advanced clinical activities

Implementation of the didactic classroom components are clearly more easily implemented than the design and availability of actual clinical activities both at the pre-doctoral and post-doctoral level. For each of these components, universities must acquire faculty with experience and expertise in supporting individuals with co-occurring needs. Implementation of the clinical elements requires the added access to actual clinics, hospitals, and other organizations that support/treat individuals with co-occurring needs. The latter can be hard to find given the issues already discussed in previous chapters.

Given the dearth of expertise with individuals with co-occurring needs and the limited number of graduate programs in some areas within each state (i.e., graduate clinical psychology programs do not exist at every university), most states will likely only have a program or two with this specialization. Ideally, specialization would occur at a larger university with an associated medical school and graduate training programs across behavioral health areas including psychiatry, psychology, and social work at a minimum. Recommended options for pursuing the development of specialized behavioral health training programs within a state's university systems might include:

1. The state UCEDD takes the lead in partnering with its university in the manner seen in Ohio and Colorado and develops an IDD specialty training option. This option could cut across multiple disciplines, particularly when the university also has an associated medical school for involvement of psychiatrists and covers a variety of behavioral health professions.

    a. UCEDD attracts and employs qualified clinicians

    b. UCEDD formally partners with university medical school, department of psychology, and department of social work minimally

    c. Specialized course requirements and electives are developed for the IDD specialization

    d. Faculty/clinicians at the UCEDD provide direct clinical opportunities within the medical school rotations and the university clinics for supervised practicum

    e. Faculty/clinicians at UCEDD offer partnership for supervision of students in other clinics that either specialize in supporting individuals with co-occurring needs or express willingness to begin supporting these individuals with the involvement and oversight of the UCEDD professional

2. The state DD agency takes the lead in partnering with either the state UCEDD or a key university with core graduate level behavioral health training programs across discipline categories.

    a. State agency may partner with the UCEDD to accomplish the activities outlined above either by the UCEDD with leadership and oversight from the state agency or in collaboration with the state agency where the state agency employs clinicians with expertise in these areas.

    b. The state agency may partner with a key university where the UCEDD is not associated with a large university within the state that supports an array of behavioral health graduate training options.

     i. The state agency may supply key faculty or adjunct staff to support the university efforts

    ii. The university will acquire and employ faculty with expertise in the area

   iii. Specialized course requirements and electives are developed for the IDD specialization

   iv. Faculty/clinicians at the university provide direct clinical opportunities within the medical school rotations and the university clinics for supervised practicum

    v. Faculty/clinicians at university offer partnership for supervision of students in other clinics that either specialize in supporting individuals with co-occurring needs or express willingness to begin supporting these individuals with the involvement and oversight of the UCEDD professional

   vi. The State agency will partner with the university to offer training via its programs/clinics

  vii. The state agency may bring the UCEDD in as a third partner to support the efforts

3. Other entities within the state take the lead in partnering with a local university with core graduate level behavioral health training programs across discipline categories. Examples of possible entities that may spearhead efforts include:

   a. State developmental disabilities council

   b. IDD provider agency organizations/groups

   c. Advocacy organizations

   d. Large health centers/hospitals

Development of Professional Mentoring Programs

Implementation of required basic coursework for all professionals and development of specialized training programs hold the best promise for the longest lasting and greatest impact on building tomorrow's professionals. However, outcomes of these efforts are years in the future. Individuals with co-occurring needs face access issues daily today and changes must begin more quickly than longer term strategies can address. Building capacity of today's professional workforce must begin even where small steps forward can occur. Professional mentoring programs need to be developed and offered with incentives.

Professional-to-Professional Mentoring

Professional-to-professional mentoring represents an idea inherently rooted in professional competence and scope of practice. Each professional when licensed or certified is expected to know and identify his/her boundaries of competence and practice; however, methods for increasing competence and capacity to serve new groups of individuals and/or use new approaches is also built into professional practice expectations. One option for achieving additional competence and capacity is use of mentoring/consultation by another professional who already has competence within the new area. Formalization of options for this type of professional-to-professional mentoring to increase capacity to support individuals with co-occurring needs can be a key component within any DD service system. This formalization may occur via a variety of avenues:

1. The state DD agency may build formal mentoring options via its clinicians and offer them to private clinicians who indicate a willingness to support individuals with co-occurring needs.

2. Advocacy groups could apply for grant funding, hire professionals with expertise, and offer mentoring to other professionals via their program.

3. Typical IDD providers who employ a professional with experience supporting individuals with IDD and behavioral/mental health needs could approach other local professionals to build local capacity.

Mentoring activities would involve consultation at key points in the assessment, plan development and treatment activities. Additionally, the mentor would be available for consultation and assistance when needed until such time as the treating professional (mentee) was comfortable proceeding independently.

Specialized Trainings and Formal Continuing Education

Every behavioral/mental health professional must complete specified numbers of continuing education activities each year to further his/her knowledge and experience and to remain independently licensed or certified to practice within his/her discipline. An initial step in building professional capacity lies in the development of appropriate and effective continuing education activities centered around treating and supporting individuals with IDD and behavioral/mental health needs. For these types of educational activities to result in increasing the professional's knowledge and comfort with offering services to individuals with co-occurring needs, careful planning of the training approach must be undertaken. Typical brief, didactic training is not likely to result in any change in actual practice. Carefully designed "in class" activities must be constructed and/or actual real practice opportunities must be developed. Incentives may be required similar to those used in North Carolina to offer mini-fellowships to physicians interested and willing to increase their capacity to treat individuals with IDD (Junczyk & Kelly, 2009). Incentives may be offered by state agencies, advocacy organizations, UCEDDs, or other large organization invested in these types of initiatives.

Examples of "in class" activities may include case scenarios with role playing or case reviews and group assessment and treatment planning recommendations. These types of activities are likely most effective in initial efforts to increase capacity – that is, broadening the acceptance of some professionals to working with individuals with co-occurring needs. It may aid in some improvements in interview and assessment approaches, familiarity with basic diagnostic modifications that might be applicable to individuals with milder IDD related challenges, and understanding and making appropriate referrals for individuals with more traditional mental health presentations and IDD. Alternatively, these in-class approaches are not likely to increase capacity or comfort with addressing the needs of individuals with more complex IDD presentations and/or more significant behavioral needs.

Development of actual "real world" training opportunities is, as one might guess, much more challenging. It involves a greater investment on the part of both the trainer and the professional trainee. It takes the ideas behind the professional-to-professional mentoring a step further. The same types of principles may be applied as those outlined in the professional-to-professional mentoring options but with a more detailed focus on the following: required assessment and treatment experiences, more formal "supervision-type" activities by a professional with training and experience serving individuals with co-occurring needs, and review and evaluation of treatment outcomes.

Development and implantation of specialized training programs may be located or co-located in several parts of the typical DD service spectrum:

1. The state UCEDD would be an appropriate point of responsibility for this type of program. With UCEDDs in some state's already taking the lead with regard to graduate training specializations, they are equipped with the professional expertise (often across disciplines) to delve into this type of continuing education approach. Specific partnerships would be needed to accomplish this effort.

   a. The UCEDD could partner with the state boards for each professional discipline and determine continuing education awarding for and documentation of these activities.

   b. The UCEDD could partner with the appropriate state agency(ies) to publicize the opportunity and to appropriately highlight benefits to clinicians in completing the additional training which may include service gaps and higher pay/incentive based options for providing certain services or serving certain populations.

2. The state DD agency may take the lead in working with several entities including the UCEDD, other university programs, and available continuing education/professional development programs within the state to offer specialized training and continuing education to professionals with regard to supporting individuals with IDD and behavioral/mental health needs. Grants may be available to the state to initiate and perhaps even maintain such a specialized training program given the lack of access in many states currently.

3. Advocacy organizations may initiate a program in a similar fashion as the state agency may via partnerships with various entities inclusive of grant opportunities.

Summary

This chapter has reviewed needed actions/recommendations to address the improvements in professional education and training. Building a network of professionals to support individuals with co-occurring needs must be moved to the forefront of efforts to address the needs of individuals with co-occurring needs. Without an adequate supply of needed professionals, the increasing demand will continue to go unmet. As with the considerations in the preceding chapter, this chapter offered a variety of options to pursue that can be initiatives by a variety of entities/programs.

Chapter 9

Where the Rubber Meets the Road: Empowerment as a Tool of Change

Individuals with IDD often require a lifetime of support. A consistent and sustained support system is associated with more positive outcomes. The additional supports needed for an individual with IDD and behavioral health needs can further strain the support system. Supporting families and caregivers must be a central feature of all systems at the larger level and within each provider who routinely supports these individuals. Families and caregivers will need support to sustain the assistance they provide and in navigating system complexities

Because individuals with IDD have needs across the lifespan, almost all individuals with IDD will have a significant support system; understanding the needs of the support system and how it interfaces with the needs of the individual must be addressed. As professionals and providers work with individuals with IDD and behavioral health needs, they must remember that recommendations and many treatment components will require family and support staff understanding, buy-in, and ability to implement. For many individuals, the behavioral health supports cannot rely on individual therapy time with a clinician solely or perhaps even as primary intervention of choice.

Family and staff burnout and stress can impact the implementation of needed behavioral supports as well as the behavioral symptom presentation of the individual supported. Behavioral health supports must include elements to address needs in this area. As we began looking at strategies to address the needs of individuals with a dual diagnosis, a key principle highlighted was person-centered thinking and planning approaches. This chapter will revisit this principle and examine how independence, empowerment, and choice play a key role in meeting the behavioral/mental health needs of individuals with IDD.

Empowering Families and Recipients

Education and outreach to families and recipients is essential for meeting all of the individual's needs. Many families feel overwhelmed when confronted with the needs of their loved ones and recipients of services may, by virtue of their IDD, have challenges in understanding and navigating through support options and programs. Several key areas of education and outreach are important.

1. When an individual has co-occurring IDD and behavioral/mental health needs, ensuring that families understand all facets of each system (public or

private) that may and should be encountered is essential. Advocacy organizations must play a key role beyond the state DD agency's programs. Knowledge and expertise in navigating all systems discussed previously must be gathered within these organizations to assist families and recipients in accessing and coordinating needed supports and treatment.

2. Families and recipients need education about the prevalence of behavioral/mental health challenges for persons with IDD. Many families presume the challenges are related to the individual's IDD (when in fact they are not) and then do not seek other needed treatment options.

Building in real choice and independence into the recipient's life can positively impact the presentation of behavioral/mental health challenges. As discussed previously in this book, behavioral challenges can occur for a variety of reasons only some of which represent significant co-existing mental health diagnoses. A portion of noted behavioral challenges for individuals with IDD can clearly be linked to lack of choice and independence for the individual. Even where clear co-existing mental health conditions are present, a focus on ensuring real choice and independence for the recipient still may positively impact the presentation of symptoms, reaction to and cooperation with needed treatment approaches, and presence or absence of other behavioral difficulties. This component must be embedded in the larger person-centered planning context discussed earlier in this book. Each individual should drive his/her life goals and vision, and all aspects of the plan should be geared at supporting the individual to move towards that vision and those goals. Treatment for behavioral health needs must consider the following to both support the individual's independence and rights as well as to achieve any degree of effectiveness:

1. Are clear strengths and opportunities being used to assist the person in moving towards his/her vision and goals?

2. Is there an understanding of how the behavioral health needs do and do not impact achievement of the vision and goals?

3. Is treatment for the behavioral health needs geared toward the person's vision and goals?

4. Are preferences and non-negotiables considered?

5. Are important personal relationships supported?

6. Is personal choice supported and are unnecessary restrictions avoided?

When the above issues are considered, there will be some individuals for whom the behavioral health issues will improve or be eliminated. For these individuals, additional professional assistance may be unnecessary. Improvements for the individual and removal of unnecessary demand for scarce services both occur when these principles are followed and implemented. For the remaining individuals, honoring the above issues and consistently revisiting them will improve implementation of supports, cooperation with needed assistance and treatment, and overall outcomes for the individual.

Support options across all programs, systems, and funding options must offer flexibility and accountability that matters to the recipient and his/her family. An individual with IDD and co-occurring behavioral/mental health needs likely presents with differing types and intensity of needs across time. Support options must be flexible enough to allow for movement into and out of intensive supports as needed to meet the individual's ever-changing needs. Crisis options must be discussed and planned for when an individual has co-occurring needs, rather than waiting until the crisis occurs. Planning for individuals with co-occurring needs must assess response to changes in need over time, crisis triage and reaction, and outcomes for the recipient. Changes should be made when an individual does not experience positive outcomes or changes.

Empowering the Support System (Paid and Unpaid)

An issue repeatedly noted throughout this book speaks to the need for support from others for many individuals with IDD throughout their lives. Some of the needed support is required to participate in and enjoy many activities and experiences in life most individuals without IDD take for granted. Family, friends, and staff who support individuals with a dual diagnosis encounter a more complex set of needs than those who support individuals with IDD only. For example, some individuals with a dual diagnosis are capable of completing most basic ADLs, but they may experience difficulties related to behavioral/mental health needs. Understanding these complex interactions and effective support options and modifications that are needed at different times is key for success. Empowering support systems encompasses at least two primary components: specialized training related to co-occurring needs and individualized training and planning to support the specific recipient(s).

Specialized Training for IDD and Behavioral/Mental Health Supports

Support persons for individuals with co-occurring needs must be provided with specialized training in supporting individuals with IDD and behavioral/mental health needs. For some time, this type of training has been referred to under the umbrella of Positive Behavior Supports (PBS) training. This author has often seen Positive Behavior Supports too narrowly defined as focused almost exclusively on more environmentally mediated behavioral challenges. While this is one basic and often foundational component of PBS, it does not capture the complexities encountered in terms of medical factors and actual co-occurring mental health conditions. Similarly, this approach often misses the needed professional involvement and therapeutic approaches necessary to meet each individual's needs. Robust and comprehensive training must be provided to support staff and offered to any interested family. Baker and colleagues (2002) noted that support staff are often ill prepared and untrained to support individuals with complex behavioral needs.

Any PBS curriculum should consider the following recommendations:

1. A modular approach allows for breaking the material into pieces that can be learned and applied by family and support staff while not overwhelming them

with the totality of all the issues one may need to consider.

2. A thorough curriculum must address the following areas:

    a. How person-centered thinking and planning set the context for behavioral/mental health supports

    b. Avoiding power struggles and balancing rights and responsibilities

    c. Identification of environmental issues that may be addressed at the family or provider level

    d. Guidelines for seeking appropriate consultation

    e. Preparing for consultation

    f. Using information from the consultation

    g. Collecting data/information and communicating with the professional

3. The focus should not emphasize what the professional will do once engaged beyond setting reasonable expectations for visits/consultations.

Training options should be offered and available to all family members engaged in supporting a loved one with co-occurring needs. Staff supporting individuals with co-occurring needs should be required to have specific additional training beyond the minimal requirements for all staff. Providers should consider appropriate pay scales for staff supporting individuals with more complex needs which may justify the additional training requirements as well as assist in staff retention for continuity of support for these individuals.

Support Team versus Professional Assistance

The family and/or support team for each recipient may be positioned to take positive action to impact behavioral challenges in some very clearly defined situations, while in others a need for professional assessment and treatment exists. Empowering the support system must include providing guidance on areas of support that the family and/or team may attempt to address with the recipient versus those necessitating professional involvement. If families and support staff are able to address some basic issues consistent with personal preferences, non-negotiables, and other known person-centered issues, then the current high demand for professional services may be positively impacted and result in only those who need that level of assessment and treatment seeking it. Tables 9 and 10 provide some guidance for consideration.

Table 9. Guidelines for Seeking Professional Assistance

Support Team	Medical Consult	Psychiatry/ Medical Psychology Consult	Psychology/BH Consult	Emergency Help
1. Known recent life changes 2. Presentation is different across situations 3. Very low level of danger	1. New behavior (never seen) 2. Sudden worsening 3. Known historical or family connection 4. Suspected/ known genetic condition 5. Signs/ symptoms of illness	1. Known MH condition with medications 2. Other odd behavior accompanies behavior 3. May need inpatient hospitalization	1. Behavior is dangerous 2. Efforts to trouble-shoot simple solutions don't work 3. Medical issue not likely/RO 4. Known MH condition not needing medication 5. Prior problem needing Professional	1. Imminent danger to self 2. Imminent danger to others 3. Major change in awareness or alertness

Table 10. Family and Staff Decision Guide

- Newly emerging behavioral challenge (never occurred before)
  - ◆ Any Major Life Changes
    - ◆ Team planning to identify challenges in recent change and needed supports
  - ◆ Look for signs of illness
    - ◆ See a medical professional
  - ◆ No specific signs illness and all other concerns ruled out
    - ◆ See a medical professional
  - ◆ No danger in behavioral presentation
    - ◆ PC planning to look at important life areas and needed changes
- Worsening of an existing behavioral challenge
  - ◆ Any Major Life Changes
    - ◆ Team planning to identify challenges in recent change and needed supports
  - ◆ If not dangerous, check preferences/relationships and access
  - ◆ If dangerous and sudden change, see medical professional
  - ◆ If previous assessment indicates relationship to medical symptoms, see medical professional
  - ◆ If known mental health diagnosis, see appropriate treating professional
    - ◆ If suspected/known genetic condition, see psychiatrist/prescriber
    - ◆ If known MH condition with medication, see psychiatrist/prescriber
    - ◆ Otherwise, see psychologist/behavioral health professional first
  - ◆ If both medical and mental health concerns are associated with behavioral challenges, see psychologist/behavioral health professional for assessment
- Existing behavioral challenge with differences across settings (i.e., Work vs home)
  - ◆ If not dangerous in either setting
    - ◆ Team discussion to look at what is working and not working in each setting
    - ◆ Make appropriate changes based on identified mismatches
  - ◆ If dangerous, see professionals as noted above (& plan for team discussion as noted once stabilized)
- Existing behavioral challenge with no improvements but low levels of dangerousness
  - ◆ Complete person centered assessment/discovery process
  - ◆ Look for opportunities for change
- Existing behavioral challenge with danger to self or others
  - ◆ If potential for danger but not imminent, see appropriate professionals as noted above
  - ◆ If danger is imminent, seek emergency services

The first consideration is whether outside assistance from a professional is needed. A second variable involves identification of the right professional assistance when needed. Recipients, families, and support teams can look at key areas within the recipient's life to target changes in support when known life changes have occurred that may warrant a temporary routine or support alteration or necessitate re-examining the support plan for modifications. Typical changes of this nature may include:

1. Death of a caregiver

2. Illness or hospitalization of a caregiver

3. Illness or hospitalization of the recipient

4. Changes in family circumstances effecting access for visits/family events/etc.

5. Changes in school or work

Similarly, different presentations across situations may indicate different implementation or availability of supports and may be corrected via the support team. The team can work to identify what is working or available in one setting that is missing in another. Ensuring access or implementation of the supports across all situations and settings may address the problem. Finally, behavioral challenges that impact the recipient but result in no real danger to the recipient or others may warrant a look by the family or support team first. Revisiting the person-centered discovery process allows the family or team to look for changes over time or new information and learning. People change and preferences, interests, and non-negotiables may change over time. Additionally, small preferences or non-negotiables may go missing with no real notice until a behavioral challenge emerges or increases. Recalibrating as a team to check how well the team is doing can often expose easy options for correcting the situation. In all other situations, professional assistance should be sought. Tables 9 and 10 can help the team determine whether a consultation is needed and what issues need to be addressed.

Once the family or team determine professional assistance is needed, preparing for a successful consultation is essential. Healthcare professionals will need to understand several key factors to provide helpful support and treatment. The family and team should consider preparation of a one page summary to bring to the consultation. Key information that must be addressed on the summary includes the following:

1. Person's vision/goals

2. Key non-negotiables

3. Description of the behavioral health needs with as much detail as possible about the new issue or change

4. Past treatment attempted and current support/treatment (if new professional)

5. Changes since last visit and any agreed upon data/information (if current professional)

6. Medical needs and treatments and any symptoms or problems currently

7. Any other new observations or other symptoms

The family and team must work with the recipient to determine what type of support is needed for the consultation. If assistance is required, the team should work to determine who is best able to offer that assistance. The person identified as best meeting the needed support should accompany the individual, not whoever happens to be scheduled to work. Ensure that a clear plan is agreed upon before leaving the consultation. Ask questions if recommendations appear inconsistent with the recipient's preferences and goals. Negotiation to reach the most effective approach may be required. Families and support staff should remember that an effective approach that cannot be implemented or that will not be agreed to by the recipient will not produce a successful outcome. Table 11 contains some examples of negotiations and rights/responsibility balances when communicating with professionals.

Table 11. Examples of Balancing-Person Centered Preferences and Needed Professional Supports

Medical Recommendation	Person-Centered Preference & Challenge	Compromise/Negotiation
Remove soda from diet	Individual drinks several Cokes per day and is now stealing from the corner grocery store to obtain Cokes	Discuss with MD the current preference and rate of accessing Coke Evaluate if substitutes (i.e., Diet Coke) may be adequate based on understanding of need: -if due to weight or sugar concerns consider diet options -if due to concerns RE caffeine consider caffeine free alternatives. Consider whether limiting or cutting back on beverages would be sufficient to meet medical need and curtail stealing
Remove sugar/desserts from diet	Individual enjoys sweets and aggression dramatically increases as family/staff attempt to remove or "take away" sugar/desserts	Discuss with MD the current preference and rate of accessing sweets Evaluate if substitutes may be adequate based on understanding of need: -try diabetic or sugar free options -do not presume that a fruit or veggie snack will suffice simply because it is a food choice Consider whether limiting or cutting back on sweets would be sufficient to meet medical need and curtail stealing

Do not complete "cosmetic" dental work as individual unlikely to "cooperate" because he/she will not "understand" the procedure	Individual has lost several teeth and continues to decline in dental hygiene and frequently points to missing teeth area in mouth	Ask behavioral health professional to work with the dentist to develop a desensitization procedure and visual cues to understand procedure Implement the plan in sequence and continue through to completion of the dental work at pace of individual
Administration of medication requiring 3 doses per day of pills by mouth to treat newly diagnosed medical condition	Individual does not cooperate well with medication particularly in pill form Individual is becoming aggression with family/staff each day due to medication need	Discuss the medication "compliance" issue with MD Determine alternatives: -medication requiring less frequent administration -liquid form -one time or infrequent injection option

Summary

This chapter has reviewed needed guidelines, tips, and tools to empower families and staff and support them in their efforts to daily support individuals with IDD. Behavioral wellness by nature requires the appropriate level of involvement and independence of the recipient. Families and support staff are the heart of each recipient's support network. Empowering recipients and families and supporting those who support them is essential to a successful outcome.

Additionally, provision of tools the recipient, family, and support team can use together to address behavioral challenges linked to problems in person centered approaches and supports and those with low risk of injury, can assist in correcting the current access to demand mismatch for professional services. The individual will then often experience increased independence, quality of life, choice and control while the support system experiences positive outcomes and decreased stress and burnout. The provider and larger system experiences a decrease in drain on already scarce resources.

Chapter 10

Summary and Conclusions

Progress has occurred in the area of behavioral health services for individuals with IDD; however, much work remains to be done. Decades following the recognition of mental health disorders and behavioral health needs for individuals with IDD, access to needed services and identification of effective service approaches continue to be a work in progress. The comorbid conditions many of these individuals experience across multiple areas within the medical, therapeutic, and behavioral realm – in addition to the IDD support needs present – result in a complex set of needs with interconnections not easily assessed or addressed.

States, programs, and professionals with expertise in this area have demonstrated that supports can be provided to these individuals with positive outcomes both in terms of symptom/behavioral presentation and quality of life improvements. Similar to the challenges faced with person-centered practices, bringing these strategies to scale across communities, states, and the nation continues to be a challenge. This book attempts to pull together key concepts and supports/programs together with a look at systems issues to identify areas where intervention and development may be fruitful. Borrowing from our individualized person-centered approaches let's take a look at some of the non-negotiables addressed:

1. Person-centered approaches must remain at the core of all support and treatment plans and approaches. Trauma Informed Care must begin to be a core feature of this approach to ensure the following:

   a. Use of person-centered approaches to avoid/prevent abuse and trauma;

   b. Proactive identification of needs related to trauma and abuse with appropriate supports identified to mitigate additional mental health risks; and

   c. Use of trauma informed practices when mental health and behavioral issues arise.

2. Remembering that IDD is a "developmental" issue at its core, key principles embedded in early intervention practices must remain throughout the lifespan, and services should not simply stop as individual's enter adulthood. Taking this approach does not mean limiting the independence of the individual with IDD. Independence should always be at the core of the goals of all supports for an individual with IDD. The incorporation of the early intervention principles simply ensures that when support from others (family or staff) is needed, that the support system can access needed information and training from the professionals and providers making recommendations. Similarly, the availability

of some supports throughout the lifespan for individuals with IDD simply ensures access when needed but does not necessitate access in the absence of an identified need. Changes that must occur in any system or program include:

    a. Expectations and methods for sustainability of a team-based approach,

    b. Needed involvement and training for family and staff as appropriate for each individual while balancing independence and support needed, and

    c. Clearly identified outcomes with expectations and methods for measurement

3. Cross systems coordination and team approaches must be developed, outlined, implemented, and monitored for effectiveness. These efforts can be looked at within any system or program and do not have to rely upon state or federal level action. The guidelines presented within this book regarding system coordination can be implemented with some success by any level within the system or by any program.

4. Education and training for professionals across disciplines must become the norm.

    a. State UCEDDs must begin to view dual diagnosis as a core issue within the framework of any successful Center of Excellence.

    b. UCEDDs and other universities must begin to look at implementation of curricula to address the needed changes within existing professional programs and to offer options for improving support coordination and support staff competencies.

    c. States, programs, and organizations supporting individuals with IDD may wish to initiate development of certification and training programs to supplement university offerings or in the absence of such offerings.

    d. Use of alternate diagnostic guidelines such as the DM-ID must become the norm for all clinicians.

5. Innovative strategies for true team work across professionals, programs, and systems must be developed.

6. Better support and education for recipients, families and support staff is essential.

    a. General guidelines and tips for families and staff must be developed by any system, program, or professional supporting individuals with IDD.

    b. Tools to assist families and staff both in the day-to-day support of individuals with IDD as well as to be effective members of a support team must be implemented.

7. Programs, professionals, advocacy organizations, and communities must look within their own spheres of influence to develop innovative and creative methods for improving the lives and health outcomes of individuals with IDD. These groups must look to state and federal programs as partners in delivering

and improving supports and services rather than as the sole owner and solution to these challenges.

This author has attempted to offer ideas and options for addressing each of the above areas. No 'one size fits all' option will work for every recipient, community, or state. Efforts were made to outline variations on recommendations and opportunities for various stakeholders to take the lead and be involved. The single most important area of consideration involves the need for all involved stakeholders to engage in the process of evaluating the system and options available to individuals with co-occurring needs in each community. There are opportunities for change, improvement, and innovation in all areas and across all entities and organizations.

References

Affordable Care Act (2010). Public Law 111-148, 124 Stat. 119.

Adams, R.C., Tapia, C., & The Council on Children with Disabilities. (2013). Early intervention, IDEA Part C services, and the medical home: Collaboration for best practice and best outcomes. *Pediatrics, 132(4)*, e1073-e1088.

Agosta, J., Fortune, J., Kimmish, M., Melda, K., & Smith, D. (2010). *Using individual budget allocations to support people with intellectual and developmental disabilities.* Portland, OR: Human Services Research Institute.

American Psychiatric Association. (2013). *Diagnostic and statistical manual for mental disorder (5th ed.).* Washington, DC: Author.

Association of University Centers on Developmental Disabilities (2011). About UCEDD. Retrieved fro http://www.aucd.org/template/page.cfm?id=667.

Baker, D.J., Blumberg, E.R., Freeman, R. & Wieseler, N.A. (2002). Can psychiatric disorders be seen as establishing operations? Integrating applied behavior analysis and psychiatry. *Mental Health Aspects of Developmental Disabilities, 5(4)*, 118-124.

Barnhill, J. (2006). Data management systems in the treatment of people with intellectual disabilities: A model for psychopharmacologists. *Mental Health Aspects of Developmental Disabilities, 9(2)*, 41-43.

Barnhill, J., & McNelis, D. (2012). Overview of intellectual/developmental disabilities. *The Journal of Lifelong Learning in Psychiatry, X(3)*, 300-307.

Barnhill, L.J. (2003). Can the DSM-IV-TR be saved for individuals with intellectual disability? *Mental Health Aspects of Developmental Disabilities, 6*, 85-99.

Barth, S., Ensslin, B. & Archibald, N. (2012). State trends and innovations in medicaid long-term services and supports. Policy Brief. Hamilton, NJ: Center for Health Care Strategies, Inc.

Beasley, J.B. & duPree, K. (2003). A systematic strategy to improve services to individuals with coexisting developmental disabilities and mental illness: National trends and the "Connecticut Blueprint." *Mental Health Aspects of Developmental Disabilities, 6(2)*, 50-90.

Beasley, J.B. & Hurley, A.D. (2007). Public systems support for people with intellectual disability and mental health needs in the United States. *Mental Health Aspects of Developmental Disabilities, 10(3)*, 118-120.

Beasley, J.B. & Kroll, J. (2002). The START/Sovner center program in Massachusetts. In R.H. Hanson, N.A Weisler, & K.C. Lakin, (Eds.), *Crisis prevention and response in the community* (pp. 97-125). Washington, DC: The American Association on Mental Retardation.

Borthwick-Duffy, S.A. (1994). Epidemiology and prevalence of psychopathology in people with mental retardation. *Journal of Consulting and Clinical Psychology, 62*, 17-27.

Braddock, D.L., Hemp, R.E., Rizzolo, M.C., Tanis, E.S., Haffee, L., & Wu, J. (2015). *The state of the states in intellectual and developmental disabilities.* Washington, DC: American Association on Intellectual and Developmental Disabilities (AAIDD)

Brookman, L., Frazie, M. Baker-Ericzen, M., Stahmer, A., Mandell, D., Haine, R., & Hough, R. (2009). Involvement of youth with autism spectrum disorders or intellectual disorders in multiple public service systems. *Journal of Mental Health Research in Intellectual Disabilities, 2(3)*, 201-219.

Burke, G. & Prindiville, K. (2011). *Medicare and Medicaid alignment: Challenges and opportunities for serving dual eligible.* Washington, DC: National Senior Citizens Law Center.

Center for Disease Control (CDC). (2014). ACE study. Retrieved from http://www.cdc.gov/violenceprevention/acestudy/index.html

Centers for Medicare and Medicaid Services (CMS) (2014a). Dual eligible beneficiaries under the Medicare and Medicaid programs. Washington, DC: United States Department of Health and Human Services.

Centers for Medicare and Medicaid Services (CMS) (2014b). HCBS setting regulations for community first choice and HCBS waivers. 42 CFR Part 441. *Federal Register, 79(11)*, Washington, DC: United States Department of Health and Human Services.

Centers for Medicare and Medicaid Services (CMS) (2014c). Medicaid Health Homes: An Overview. Retrieved from http://www.medicaid.gov/state-resource-center/medicaid-state-technial-assistance/health-homes-technical-assistance/downloads/medicaid-health-homes-overview.pdf.

Centers for Medicare and Medicaid Services (CMS) (2015). State operation manual: Appendix J-guidelines for surveyors of intermediate care facilities for individuals with intellectual disabilities. Retrieved from http://www.cms.gov/Regulations-and-Guidance/Guidance/Manuals/Downloads/som107ap_j_intermcare.pdf.

Charlot, L. (2014) A medical home pilot program for individuals with intellectual disabilities and/or autism spectrum disorders and mental health disorders: The UMASS Collaborative Care Model. *NADD Bulletin, 16(6)*, 122-123.

Charlot, L. & Beasley, J.B. (2013). Intellectual disability and mental health: United States-Based research. *Journal of Mental Health Research in Intellectual Disabilities, 6(2)*, 74-105.

Chowdhury, M. & Benson, B.A. (2011). Deinstitutionalization and quality of life of individuals with intellectual disability: A review of the international literature. *Journal of Policy and Practice in Intellectual Disabilities, 8,* 256-265.

Cooper, R. (2013). *Medicaid residential options for people with autism and other developmental disabilities.* Alexandria, VA: National Association of State Directors of Developmental Disabilities Services..

Cooper, S.A., Smiley, E., Morrison, J., Williamson, A. & Allan, I. (2007). Mental ill-health in adults with intellectual disabilities: Prevalence and associated factors. *British Journal of Psychiatry, 190,* 27-35.

Deb, S., Clarke, D., & Unwin, G. (2006). *Using medication to manage behavior problems among adults with a learning disability: Quick reference guide (QRG),* University of Birmingham, MENCAP, The Royal College of Psychiatrists, London, ISBN 0855370947. www.Id-medication.bham.ac.uk

Deb, S., Holt, G., & Bouras, N. (2004). Practice guidelines for the assessment and diagnosis of mental health problems of adults with intellectual disability. *NADD Bulletin, 7(1),* 15-16.

Dekker, M. & Koot, H.M. (2003). DSM-IV disorders in children with borderline to moderate intellectual disability: Prevalence and impact. *Journal of the American Academy of Child and Adolescent Psychiatry, 42,* 915-922.

Developmental Disabilities Assistance and Bill of Rights Act (2000). Public Law 106-402. 114 Stat. 1677.

Division of Early Childhood Education. (2014). *Recommended practices in early intervention and early childhood education.* Council for Exceptional Children.

Dorfman, D.A. & Awmiller, C. (2003). Litigating system reform cases on behalf of individuals with developmental disabilities and mental health needs. *Mental Health Aspects of Developmental Disabilities, 6(20,* 42-49.

Dunst, C.J. & Trivette, C.M. (2009). Using research evidence to inform and evaluate early childhood intervention practices. *Topics in Early Childhood Special Education, 29,* 40-52.

Emerson, E. (1995). *Challenging behaviour: Analysis and intervention in people with learning disabilities.* Cambridge, UK: Cambridge University Press.

Esbensen, A. J., Rojahn, J., Aman, M. G., & Ruedrich, S. (2003). Reliability and validity of an assessment instrument for anxiety, depression, and mood among individuals with mental retardation. *Journal of Autism and Developmental Disorders, 33(6),* 617-629.

Fletcher, R.J., Loeschen, E., Stavrakaki, C., & First, M. (eds) (2007). *Diagnostic manual-Intellectual disabilities: A clinical guide for mental disorders in persons with intellectual disabilities.* Kingston, NY: NADD Press.

Grey, I., Pollard, J., McClean, B., MacAuley, N., & Hastings, R. (2014). Prevalence of psychiatric diagnoses and challenging behavior in a community-based population of adults with intellectual disabilities. *Journal of Mental Health Research in Intellectual Disabilities, 3(4),* 210-222.

Health Research and Services Administration. (2014). School-based health centers. Retrieved from http://hrsa.gov/ourstories/schoolhealthcenters/.

Hierstein, D. & Bradley, V. (2014). What do NCI data reveal about individuals with intellectual and developmental disabilities who need behavioral support? Retrieved from http://www.nationalcoreindicators.org/upload/core-indicators/NCI_DataBrief_MAY2014_ADDENDUM_04_20_15.pdf.

Holden, B. & Gittleson, J.P. (2003). Prevalence of psychiatric symptoms in adults with mental retardation and challenging behavior. *Research in Developmental Disabilities, 24,* 323-332.

Horovitz, M., Shear, S., Mancini, L.M., & Pellerito, V.M. (2014). The relationship between AXIS I pathology and quality of life in adults with mild to moderate intellectual disabilities. *Research in Developmental Disabilities, 35,* 137-143

Hughes, K., Bellis, M.A., Jones, L., Wood, S., Bates, G., Eckley, L.,...Officer, A. (2012a). Prevalence and risk of violence against adults with disabilities: A systematic review and meta-analysis of observational studies. *Lancet, 379 (9826),* 1621-1629.

Hughes, K., Bellis, M.A., Jones, L., Wood, S., Bates, G., Eckley, L.,... Officer, A. (2012b). Prevalence and risk of violence against children with disabilities: a systematic review and meta-analysis of observational studies. *Lancet, 380(9845),* 899-907.

Individuals with Disabilities Education Act (IDEA) (2004). Act 20 U.S.C. 1400 et seq.

Iverson, J.C. & Fox, R.A. (1989). Prevalence of psychopathology among mentally retarded adults. *Research in Developmental Disabilities, 10,* 77-83.

Jacobstein, D.M., Stark, D.R., & Laygo, R.M. (2007). Creating responsive systems for children with co-occurring developmental and emotional disorders. *Mental Health Aspects of Developmental Disabilities, 10(3),* 91-98.

Jennings, D., Hanline, M.F., & Woods, J. (2012). Using routines-based interventions in early childhood special education. *Dimensions of Early Childhood, 40(2),* 13-23.

Junczyk, I. & Kelly, B. (2009). Embedding developmental disabilities into medical training. *North Carolina Medical Journal, 70(6),* 556-560.

Kaiser Commission on Medicaid and the Uninsured (2009). How is the Affordable Care Act leading to changes in Medicaid long term supports and services today? States adoption of six LTSS options. Washington, DC: The Henry J. Kaiser Family Foundation.

Kastner, T.A. & Walsh, K.K. (2012). Health care for individuals with intellectual and developmental disabilities: An integrated dd health home model. *International Review of Research in Developmental Disabilities, 43,* 1-40.

Keesler, J.M. (2014). A call for the implementation of trauma informed care among individuals among intellectual and developmental disability organizations. *Journal of Policy and Practice in Intellectual Disabilities, 11(1)*, 34-42.

King, K., Jordan, A., Mazurek, E., Earle, K., Earle, E., & Runham, A. (2009). Assertive community treatment-developmental disabilities: The hyphen was the easy part. *Mental Health Aspects of Developmental Disabilities, 12(1)*, 1-7.

Lakin, K.C., Doljanic, R., Taub, S., Chiri, G., & Byun, S. (2007). Adults with dual diagnosis of intellectual and psychiatric disability receiving Medicaid home and community based services (HCBS) and ICF/MR recipients in six states. *Mental Health Aspects of Developmental Disabilities, 10(3)*, 78-90.

Lehrer, D.L. & Ott, D. (2009). Treatment outcomes for individuals with developmental disabilities and challenging behavior and psychiatric hospitalization referred to an interdisciplinary clinic. *Mental Health Aspects of Developmental Disabilities, 12(1)*.

Lysol, J.S. (2009). CANS and ANSA instruments: History and application. In J.S. Lyons & D.A. Weiner (Eds.), *Behavioral health care: Assessment, service planning, and total clinical outcomes management.* Kingston, NJ: Civic Research Institute.

Marston, G. M., Perry, D. W., & Roy, A. (1997). Manifestations of depression in people with intellectual disability. *Journal of Intellectual Disability Research, 41*(6), 476-480.

Matson, J.L. & Bamburg, J.W. (1998). Reliability of the Assessment of Dual Diagnosis (ADD). *Research in Developmental Disabilities, 19*, 89-95.

Matson, J.L., Gardner, W.I., Coe, D.A., & Sovner, R. (1991). A scale for evaluating emotional disorders in severely and profoundly mentally retarded persons: Development of the Diagnostic Assessment for the Severely Handicapped (DASH) scale. *British Journal of Psychiatry, 159*, 404-409.

Matson, J.L., & Shoemaker, M.E. (2011). Psychopathology and intellectual disabilities. *Current Opinions in Psychiatry, 24*, 367-371.

Matson, J.L. & Williams, L.W. (2014). The making of a field: The developmental of comorbid psychopathology research in persons with intellectual disabilities and autism spectrum disorders. *Research in Developmental Disabilities, 35*, 234-238.

May, M.E. & Kennedy, C.H. (2010). Health and problem behavior among people with intellectual disabilities. *Behavior Analysis in Practice, 3(2)*, 4-12.

McMorris, C.A., Weiss, J.A., Cappelletti, G. & Lunsky, Y. (2013). Family and staff perspectives on service use for individuals with intellectual disabilities in crisis. *Journal of Mental Health Research in Intellectual Disabilities, 6(1)*, 14-28.

Mindham, J., & Espie, C. A. (2003). Glasgow Anxiety Scale for people with an Intellectual Disability (GAS-ID): Development and psychometric properties of a new measure for use with people with mild intellectual disability. *Journal of Intellectual Disability Research, 47*(1), 22-30.

Mohr, C., Tonge, B. J., & Einfeld, S. L. (2005). The development of a new measure for the assessment of psychopathology in adults with intellectual disability. *Journal of Intellectual Disability Research, 49*(7), 469-480.

Moseley, C. (2003). Coordinating services for people with co-occurring mental illness and developmental disabilities. Project Technical Report, April, 2003. Alexandria, VA: National Association of State Directors of Developmental Disability Services.

Moseley, C. (2004). Survey on state strategies for supporting individuals with co-existing conditions. Project Technical Report, October, 2004. Arlington, VA: National Association of State Directors of Developmental Disability Services.

Moseley, C. (2012). Population based strategies for supporting people with co-occurring mental illness and intellectual and developmental disabilities. Presentation at Olmstead Policy Academy, September, 2012. Arlington, VA: National Association of State Directors of Developmental Disability Services.

Moss, S. (2001). Psychiatric Disorders in adults with mental retardation. *International Review of Research in Mental Retardation, 24*, 211-243.

Moss, S., Ibbotson, B., Prosser, H., Goldberg, D., Patel, P., & Simpson, N. (1997). Validity of the PAS-ADD for detecting psychiatric symptoms in adults with learning disability (mental retardation). *Social Psychiatry and Psychiatric Epidemiology, 32*(6), 344-354.

Moss, S., Prosser, H., Costello, H., Simpson, N., Patel, P., Rowe, S.,…Hatton, C. (1998). Reliability and validity of the PAS-ADD Checklist for detecting psychiatric disorders in adults with intellectual disability. *Journal of Intellectual Disability Research, 42*(2), 173-183.

Munir, K.M., (2009). Psychiatry of intellectual and developmental disabilities in the U.S.: Time for a new beginning. *Psychiatry, 8*, 448-452.

Myrbakk, E. & von Tetzchner, S. (2008). The prevalence of behavioral problems among people with intellectual disability living in community settings. *Journal of Mental Health Research in Intellectual Disabilities, 1*, 205-222.

National Association for the Dually Diagnosed (NADD). (2013). Including individuals with intellectual/developmental disabilities and co-occurring mental illness: Challenges that must be addressed in health care reform. Retrieved from http://thenadd.org/wp-content/uploads/2013/10/NADD-Position-Statement-on-letterhead.pdf.

National Association of School Psychologists. (2010). RE exemption J-3 of the Proposed Model Act for State Licensure of Psychologists. NASP Press.

National Association of State Directors of Developmental Disability Services (NASDDDS). (2014). What do NCI data reveal about individuals with intellectual and developmental disabilities who need behavior support? *NCI Data Brief, May 2014.*

National Council on Behavioral Health. (2011). Screening tools. Retrieved from http://www.integration.samhsa.gov.

National Council on Disability. (2013). Medicaid managed care for people with disabilities: Policy and implementation considerations for state and federal policymakers. Washington D.C.: Author.

National Dissemination Center for Children with Disabilities (2014). Categories of disability under IDEA. Retrieved from http://nichcy.org/disability/categories.

Perez, T.E. (2012). Olmstead enforcement update: Using the ADA to promote community inclusion. Washington, DC: US Department of Justice.

Pfadt, A. & Wheeler, D.J. (2006). Applying a continuous quality improvement model to make data-based clinical decisions. *Mental Health Aspects of Developmental Disabilities, 9(2)*, 44-53.

Regents of the University of Colorado. (2014). JFK Developmental Disabilities University Center of Excellence in DD Rotation. Retrieved from http://www.UCoCenter.edu/academics/colleges/medicalshool/departments/familymed/education/predocpsych/Pages/JFKDevelopmentalDisabilities.aspx.

Reiss, S. (1982). Psychopathology and mental retardation: Survey of a developmental disabilities mental health program. *Mental Retardation, 20,* 128-132.

Reiss, S. (1990). Prevalence of dual diagnosis in community-based day programs in the Chicago metropolitan area. *American Journal on Mental Deficiency, 94,* 575-585.

Reiss, S., Levitan, G.W., & McNally, R.J. (1982). Emotionally disturbed mentally retarded people: An underserved population. *American Psychologist, 37,* 361-367.

Reiss, S. Levitan, G.W., & Szysko, J. (1982). Emotional disturbance and mental retardation: Diagnostic overshadowing. *American Journal of Mental Deficiency, 86(6),* 567-574.

Reiss, S. & Szyszko, J. (1983). Diagnostic overshadowing and professional experience with mentally retarded persons. *American Journal of Mental Deficiency, 87(4),* 396-402.

Reiss, S. & Valenti-Hein, D. (1994). Development of psychopathology rating scale for children with mental retardation. *Journal of Consulting and Clinical Psychology, 62,* 28-33.

Rojahn, J., Matson, J. L., Lott, D., Esbensen, A. J., & Smalls, Y. (2001). The Behavior Problems Inventory: An instrument for the assessment of self-injury, stereotyped behavior, and aggression/destruction in individuals with developmental disabilities. *Journal of Autism and Developmental Disorders, 31(6),* 577-588.

Rojahn, J., Matson, J.L., Naglieri, J.A., & Mayville, E. (2004). Relationship between psychiatric conditions and behavior problems among adults with mental retardation. *American Journal on Mental Retardation, 109,* 21-33.

Rosenbaum, J.D. (2008). The CMS Medicaid Targeted Case Management Rule: Impact for Special Needs Services Providers and Programs. Center for Health Care Strategies, Inc, Issue Brief. Retrieved from http://www.chcs.org/media/CMS_Medicaid_Targeted_Case_Management_Rule.pdf.

Royal College of Psychiatry. (2001). *DC-LD (Diagnostic criteria for psychiatric disorders for use with adults with learning disabilities/mental retardation)*. London: Gaskell Press.

Ruedrich, S., Dunn, J., Schwartz, S., & Nordgreen, L. (2007). Psychiatric education in intellectual disabilities: One programs ten years of experience. *Academic Psychiatry, 31*, 430-434.

Schwartz, S.A., Ruedrich, S.L., & Dunn, J.E. (2005). Psychiatry in mental retardation and developmental disabilities: A training for psychiatric residents. *Mental Health Aspects of Developmental Disabilities, 8(1)*, 13-21.

Schiffman, D. & Biagoli, R. (2014). A comparison of the roles and functions of psychiatrists and psychologists in treating the dually-diagnosed: Implications for a more inclusive treatment methodology. *NADD Bulletin, 16(6)*, 118-120.

Sevin, J., Bowers-Stephens, C., & Crafton, C. (2003). Psychiatric disorders in adolescents with developmental disabilities: Longitudinal data on diagnostic disagreement in 150 clients, *Child Psychiatry and Human Development, 34(2)*, 147-163.

Siegel, M., Doyle, K., Chemelski, B., Payne, D., Ellsworth, N., Harmon, J.,… Lubetsky, M. (2011). Specialized inpatient psychiatry units for children with autism and developmental disorders: A United States survey. *Journal of Autism and Developmental Disorders, 42(9)*, 1863-1869.

Smith, S. (2014). Behavior support: It's not just a job. It's a mission. *NADD Bulletin, 16(6)*, 111-114.

Smull, M.W., Bourne, M.L., & Sanderson, H. (2010). Best practice, expected practice, and challenge of scale. Retrieved from http://www.nasddds.org/uploads/documents/BestPracticeExpectedPractice1.pdf.

Sobsey, D. & Doe, T. (1991). Patterns of sexual abuse and assault. *Sexuality and Disability, 9* (3), 243-259.

Sobsey, D., Wells, D., Lucardie, R. & Mansell, S. (1995). *Violence & disability: An annotated bibliography*. Baltimore: Brookes Publishing.

Sovner, R. (1986). Limiting factors in the use of DSM-III criteria with mentally ill/mentally retarded persons. *Psychopharmacology Bulletin, 22*, 1055-1059.

Spotts, S. (2012). DDRS Health Home Initiative: Meeting the triple aim through care coordination. Retrieved from http://ckfindiana.org/files/calendar/IN%20DDRS%20Health%20Home%20Overview%207%202012.pdf.

Substance Abuse and Mental Health Services Administration (SAMHSA) (2013). Report to Congress on the Nation's Substance Abuse and Mental Health Workforce Issues. Retrieved from http://www.store.samhsa.gov/shin/content/PEP13-RTC-BHWORK/PEP13-RTC-BHWORK.pdf.

Substance Abuse and Mental Health Services Administration (SAMHSA) (2015). Trauma informed approach and trauma-specific interventions. Retrieved from http://www.samhsa.gov/nctic/trauma-interventions.

Sullivan, P.M. (2009). Violence exposure among children with disabilities. *Clinical Child and Family Psychology Review, 12(2),* 196-210.

Sullivan, P. & Knutson, J. (2000). Maltreatment and disabilities: A population-based epidemiological study. *Child Abuse & Neglect, 24* (10), 1257-1273.

Thaler, N., Moseley, C., Cooper, R., & LeBeau, K. (2008). How to manage in an economic downturn. Washington, DC: National Association of State Directors of Developmental Disability Services.

The Ohio State University Nisonger Center. (2014). Psychology Graduate Training in Intellectual and Developmental Disabilities. Retrieved from http://www.nisonger.osu.edu/iddpsych.

Unwin, G., & Deb, S. (2008). Use of medication for the management of behavior problems among adults with intellectual disabilities: a clinicians' consensus survey. *American Journal on Mental Retardation, 113 (1),* 19-31.

U.S. Department of Health and Human Services. (2005). *The Surgeon General's call to action to improve the health and wellness of persons with disability.* Washington D.C.: Author.

U.S. Public Health Services. (2002). *Closing the gap: A national blueprint for improving the health of individuals with mental retardation, report of the Surgeon General's conference on health disparities and mental retardation.* Washington, DC: Author.

Viecili, M.A., MacMullen, J.A., Weiss, J.A., & Lunsky, Y. (2010). Predictors of psychology graduate student interest in field of developmental disabilities. *Journal of Mental Health Research in Intellectual Disabilities, 3(4),* 190-201.

Wand, T. (2012). Investigating the evidence for the effectiveness of risk assessment in mental health care. *Issues in Mental Health Nursing, 33,* 2-7.

Index